The West Highland White Terrier

Jill Arnel

The West Highland White Terrier

Project Team
Editor: Heather Russell-Revesz
Copy Editor: Carrie Hornbeck
Design: Lundquist Design
Series Design: Mada Design
Series Originator: Dominique De Vito

T.F.H. Publications
President/CEO: Glen S. Axelrod
Executive Vice President: Mark E. Johnson
Publisher: Christopher T. Reggio
Production Manager: Kathy Bontz

T.F.H. Publications, Inc.
One TFH Plaza
Third and Union Avenues
Neptune City, NJ 07753

06 07 08 09   1 3 5 7 9 8 6 4 2

Library of Congress Cataloging-in-Publication Data
Arnel, Jill.
 The West Highland white terrier / Jill Arnel.
   p. cm.
 Includes index.
 ISBN 0-7938-3643-3 (alk. paper)
 1. West Highland white terrier. I. Title.
 SF429.W4A76 2005
 636.755—dc22

The Leader In Responsible Animal Care For Over 50 Years!™
www.tfhpublications.com

TABLE OF CONTENTS

HISTORY
OF THE WEST HIGHLAND WHITE TERRIER

The Latin name for *dog* is *Canis familiaris*. The generic *Canis* stands for the dentition it shares with its cousins: wolves, coyotes, and jackals; the species, *familiaris*, stands for the characteristic eye structure that lacks the slit pupils of its feral cousins. The domestic dog, like the wolf (*Canis lupus*) and the coyote (*Canis latrans*), has a total of 78 chromosomes, explaining why domestic dogs are biologically able to breed with wolves and coyotes. The dog's 78 chromosomes account for the amazing physical diversity throughout dogdom. Only the minutest genetic difference separates the statuesque Afghan Hound from the diminutive West Highland White Terrier.

Appearances range from that of the plush-coated, heavy-shedding Norwegian Elkhound to the hairless Chinese Crested and everything in between. Shaving each down to the skin (not recommended) would reveal a basic similar structure; however, the differences in size, coat type, eye color, ear style, and carriage vary greatly. Add evolution and adaptation to this cauldron of diversification, and you get dogs in all their numerous forms. The world's many terrains and climates, along with human selection, influenced which dogs would become the first symbiotic companion animals.

EARTH DOGS

Terriers originate from the British Isles. The word *terrier* derives from the Latin *terra,* which means "earth." So these are "earth dogs," dogs selectively bred to go to ground to bolt or capture prey, typically foxes and badgers. Keenly intelligent and truculent—sometimes to a fault—they have the moxie to fight to the end rather than retreat unvictorious.

Terriers, as a rule, bark a lot, but this is an asset to performing their job. Stentorian barks, belying their relatively small size, often force their quarry from its hole, for easy elimination.

WESTIE ORIGINS

The Westie appears to be native to Argyllshire, Scotland. As for its origins, some contend that the modern Westie is simply a Cairn Terrier that took a detour. Cairns and Westies appear to be closest in type to the original Scotch Terrier, and some opine that the Westie descends from the white, sandy, and cream-colored Cairn Terriers. Still, the Westie's shorter back, heavier bone, and more refined grooming distinguishes it from the "tidied dishevelment" of its Cairn cousins. A gay, "noon" tail carriage contrasts with its cousin's "one or two o'clock" set.

Another hypothesis establishes the Westie's birthright as an original ancient terrier—not as descended from the Cairn Terrier, per se, but in fact on equal footing—one and the same. Only later did a "color war" cause them to follow divergent paths.

BREED HISTORY IN SCOTLAND AND ENGLAND

The first known mention of the West Highland White Terrier appears in records that date back to King James I in the late 1500s and the 1600s, when the monarch shipped six little white "earthdogges" from Argyllshire, Scotland to the French king. Many believe that these were ancestors to today's Westie. However, the color of these "earthdogges" is debatable. Mrs. May Pacey, one of the great pioneering Westie breeders, refers to these dogs in her 1963 book, but Bryan Cummins, in *Terriers of Scotland and Ireland,* suggests that Mrs. Pacey might have woven into the story a bit of wishful thinking. Logical evidence suggests that these "earthdogges" were early Scotch Terriers, but since colored ones were then favored, it's unlikely that these voyagers were white. In fact, the original records contain no color description whatsoever. However, these émigrés were close in type to the original Scotch Highland Terrier—the progenitors of both the Cairn Terrier and the West Highland White Terrier.

Three Varieties of Westies

Along the way in the history and breeding of the Westie, several different varieties were developed.

The Poltalloch Variety

Clearer documentation of the Westie's history began in the early 1800s with the Malcolm family of Poltalloch in Argyllshire. Colonel Edward Donald Malcolm of Poltalloch, generally credited as the breed's originator, took great pains to establish a hardy type of small white-coated terriers who would be well suited to the difficult terrain of the Western Highlands, breeding for exceptional working and hunting ability. For a century before, the Malcolm clan had been among the few who bred both white and colored terriers. They recognized the value of the white terriers: They were less likely than their darker kennel mates to blend in with their surroundings.

Like other lairds of the time, Colonel Malcolm kept only the best working dogs—and his were both white and colored. It was an unfortunate hunting accident that initially led Malcolm to start breeding white terriers exclusively. During a hunt, Colonel Malcolm mistook a favorite reddish

On the northern shore of Loch Crinan in the Argyllshire rests the estate where the modern Westie was born, and Duntrune Castle, where the current chief of clan MacCallum/Malcolm—Robin Neill Malcolm—a direct descendent of Colonel Malcolm, resides.

brown dog for a fox, and shot it. Devastated by his mistake, he vowed never to allow this to happen again, thereafter keeping only the cream-colored or white terriers. This put him at odds with the then-popular superstitious belief (to which the Malcolm family never quite subscribed) that white dogs were inherently inferior to their darker littermates. White dogs were often destroyed at birth because of this superstition, but luckily, the attempt to drive them into oblivion was unsuccessful. Otherwise, when, if ever, would they have had the opportunity to prove their mettle?

The Roseneath Variety

Another breeder of white terriers who figures prominently into the contemporary Westie development was the Duke of Argyll of Roseneath, whose gamekeeper, George Clark, was breeding a strain of terriers similar to the Poltalloch. These were reputed to have whiter coats of softer texture than Colonel Malcolm's terriers. However, the names Roseneath and Poltalloch were often used interchangeably until the turn of the twentieth century.

Colonel Malcolm did not breed to the Roseneath stock, as he was not fond of the longer "Skye heads." But some crossing between the two types occurred nonetheless.

The Pittenweem Variety

Dr. Americ Flaxman, of Fife on the coastal area of the Firth of Forth, began breeding white dogs primarily out of a Scottish Terrier bitch who, when bred to other white Highland Terriers, consistently threw white puppies. Possessing "linty" white coats and exceptional black pigmentation on noses, pads, and eye rims, they essentially resembled white Scotties. Other strains produced cream-colored dogs with hard coats.

Flaxman's dogs were known as Pittenweem Terriers. Flaxman and Colonel Malcolm were at odds regarding their visions as to what comprised a proper head, but this disagreement over "type" did not completely curtail interbreeding among these dogs (providing a plausible argument for the slightly closer ear set of the Westie compared to the Cairn).

Eventually, the Pittenweem Terrier faded into oblivion. No Scottish Terrier breeders wanted white dogs, nor did admirers of Poltalloch's more moderate type want the exaggerated appearance of a Scottie.

The Poltalloch Prevails

All three varieties were entered at dog shows in England in the nineteenth century. Judges, however, came to favor the shorter head and muzzle of Colonel Malcolm's Poltalloch dogs. The Duke of Argyll's Roseneaths fared somewhere in the middle, but Flaxman's Pittenweem Terriers' exaggerated heads were quickly deemed serious faults. So Malcolm's type—the Poltalloch—prevailed, and remains closest to what survives today.

In fact, Colonel Malcolm came up with the descriptive name for the breed: West Highland White Terrier, and he remained a force in unifying the various factions to contribute significantly to the breed's standardization. Through his diplomacy, the West Highland White Terrier Club of Scotland—of which he was the first president—was formed. A club in England followed, and by 1907 there were classes for Westies at Crufts, England's premier dog show.

Modern Westie Breeders In England

Mrs. Cyril (May) Pacey and her famous "Wolveys" figure prominently into the breed's lore. Starting early in the Westie's official history, Mrs. Pacey exerted worldwide influence for about fifty years before her death in 1963. Through her unparalleled dedication, she became an authority on the breed.

Ch. Wolvey Piper was her first official Champion of Record, in 1911. The period between 1920 and 1939 yielded 125 Westie champions: A full quarter of them were of Mrs. Pacey's breeding, including one of the most admired show bitches, Ch. Wolvey Pintail. With an eye to the integrity and perpetuation of the breed, Mrs. Pacey shared her finest stock worldwide to ensure the welfare of the terriers she loved. Sixty-plus Wolvey Westies became champions, and there is Wolvey blood behind many top winners.

Mrs. Pacey survived the cessation of showing (1916) and breeding (1917) that accompanied World War I, and slogged through the lean years of World War II, when rations and the dangers of far-reaching hostilities continued to threaten the hobby of keeping purebred dogs. During the WWI food shortages, she reluctantly put down fifteen of her dogs. By 1939, showing was officially restricted, but breeding remained legal. So Mrs. Pacey cannily sent some of her best stock abroad, which greatly contributed to the breed's survival. She kept a few dogs for herself, kenneled separately to ensure the survival in case her kennel was bombed. All survived, except for one—tragically run over by an army truck. Without Mrs. Pacey's selfless vision, the breed would not thrive as it does today.

Starting around 1946, shows resumed and the breed flourished. A show on July 11, 1946 ushered in a new era, with an astonishing entry of 225 Westies. And in 1950, a Westie named Shiningcliff Simon won Best Terrier honors at the prestigious Crufts show. The resumption of all-breed shows sparked a renaissance in purebred dogs in general and—with these favorably timed wins—in the West Highland White Terrier specifically.

The modern-day Westie star was Eng. Ch. Olac Moonpilot—owned, bred, and handled by Derek Tattersall. In 1990 "Paddy" won Best in Show at Crufts.

Westie Winners

- In 1860 a "white scotch terrier" was a winner at a dog show in Birmingham, England.
- Shown in October 1905 as a West Highland White Terrier, Morvan, at a mere seven and a half months old, won a Championship Certificate (CC); Morvan later become a champion.
- By 1907 there were three West Highland White Terrier champions.

BREED HISTORY IN THE UNITED STATES

In 1906 the Westie debuted in the United States as the Roseneath Terrier, but soon that name would be supplanted by the current name, West Highland White Terrier. By 1908 the breed received official listing in the American Kennel Club (AKC) Stud Book. The West Highland White Terrier Club of America formed and was admitted to the AKC in 1909. On September 21, 1909, the West Highland White Terrier Club of America was founded on the East Coast with a charter membership of fourteen. Three months later, the club submitted a breed standard to the AKC, which essentially cloned the British standard. Since then, little has changed.

Crufts winner "Paddy" made his mark in the dog world as a sire, and as a champion show dog to boot.

Champions in America

At first, most of the Westie champions were combinations of both imports and American-bred dogs. Popularity came gradually, but things would change in 1942 when Ch. Wolvey Pattern of Edgerstone (of Mrs. Pacey's previously mentioned Wolvey Westies, exported to the States during World War II) took Best of Show at Westminster, the first of two Westies ever to have earned the honor. This high-status win signaled the beginning of the breed's popularity. In the early 1960s, registrations of the breed reached upwards of a thousand.

Mixed-Heritage Terriers

For generations Cairn Terriers and West Highland White Terriers were interbred and often littermates. And in the early 1900s, Cairn Terriers and Westies continued to be interbred and sorted according to color.

Finally, in 1917, the AKC began refusing to register any Cairn Terrier with a Westie within the first three generations of its pedigree—and vice versa. The two breeds parted ways for good and became more distinct from each other. England's Kennel Club (KC) followed suit in 1924—seven years after the AKC decreed the terriers of "mixed heritage" ineligible.

In 1962, Ch. Elfinbrook Simon smashed records by winning 12 Best in Shows in America and 3 in Canada. In 1962, Simon won the National Specialty. When he won Westminster in 1963, the advent of TV broadcasting further boosted the breed's popularity, and Westie registrations tripled in the decade that followed. Regional clubs mushroomed throughout the United States. With an astonishing 27 Best in Shows, Simon set a new record for the breed, which still remains.

Eng. Ch. Cruben Dexter, owned by Barbara Worcester Keenan of Wishing Well Kennels, became a champion in Canada, and won the breed's first back-to-back Westie Best in Shows in the United States in 1954. Mrs. Keenan later became a respected AKC all-breed judge. In 1960, Wishing Well import Ch. Symmetra Snip was the first Westie to win a Best in Show at the National Terrier Show at Montgomery County. Among the wins of Wishing Well Kennel's Am. Can. Ch. Whitebriar Journeyman was one under Mr. Alva Rosenberg, the legendary "dean of judges"—a gentleman of unparalleled integrity and reputation.

Furthering the Westie cause in America, Bea and John T. Marvin were among the greatest stewards, promoters, and educators ever to grace the breed. Bea oversaw the breeding program while John concentrated on observing, studying, and writing. Both were esteemed AKC judges as well.

Breeding Trends

Breeder trends in the United States have changed over the years. While individual breeders may have strong lines, the general decline of the larger kennels makes it difficult to follow any particular line in the United States. By the turn of the twenty-first century, many breeders were beginning to keep fewer than ten dogs. Furthermore, possibly due to the size of the United States, breeding has evolved to become

Influential Westies

- In the 1930s, Furzfield Piper, no star in the show ring, became a great Westie producer and influential sire, proving that not all "lesser showmen" produce poorly. (Nor are all "showstoppers" great producers.)
- The first Westie to win a US show was named Talloch (1908). But the first American champion was a British import, Cream of the Skies.

Ch. Elfinbrook Simon, shown here in a 1968 ad from Terrier Type, *had a huge impact on the breed in the United States.*

"I CAME BACK"

CH. ELFINBROOK SIMON
BEST IN SHOW
WEST HIGHLAND WHITE TERRIER CLUB
OF SOUTHERN CALIFORNIA
1968

"And we're glad you did!"
WISHING WELL KENNELS

more regional, rather than national, in character. Washington breeder Sandy Davis cites as a possible rationale the longer distances people have to travel in the West. "Or maybe we are just too independent," she quips (terrierlike).

Breed numbers have swollen in recent years. The proliferation of Westies in television and print ads continues to augment their popularity. However, without the Westie's delightful personality, no amount of advertising could sustain the breed's place in human hearts.

A few long-lived influential kennels continue to produce many show, companion, and performance dogs. Two examples are Donnybrook Kennels in Baltimore, Maryland, and Dawn's Highland Scots Kennels in Pennsylvania. Billye and Tom Ward's Donnybrook Kennels has produced more than 100 champions and one known and admired for their longevity. Dawn Martin has bred more than 70 conformation champions, and her kennels are distinguished for breeding for both conformation and performance.

BREED CLUBS

Westie breed clubs help maintain the standard and the integrity of their breed. They foster dialogue and study and gather information and history in pursuit of "the perfect Westie." They provide and sponsor recreational activities and share important knowledge. Furthermore, Westie enthusiasts are very willing to help newcomers to the breed. Not to be overlooked, Westie clubs offer many opportunities for friendship, based on mutual love for a very special breed.

The West Highland White Terrier Club of America (WHWTCA), the central and only official AKC national club for Westies, is unquestionably the best clearinghouse in the United States for Westie information. The WHWTCA is dedicated to Westie health, welfare, preservation, enhancement, and stewardship and unites serious breeders and fanciers alike who are concerned with all things Westie.

This national organization, with the help of various satellite regional clubs, supports the breeding of healthy, fine-tempered dogs, takes care of its rescues, and is the highest-level sanctioned Westie club approved by the AKC. There are currently 21 sanctioned regional West Highland White Terrier clubs in the United States, each an independent entity under the auspices of the parent club. Many have websites that provide a cornucopia of information about Westies.

Can. Ch. Celtic Legacy with owner David Gignac.

CHARACTERISTICS

OF THE WEST HIGHLAND WHITE TERRIER

The West Highland White Terrier's fashionable tidy white coat and chic appearance belies his "of course wearing white after Labor Day is OK" independence. For these free-spirited and iconoclastic terriers, certain rules were made to be broken. They may look pure and angelic, but they are far from trivial froufrou dogs willing to sit around and drink tea from bone china with pinkies daintily curled upward (assuming they had them).

Colonel Edward Malcolm (arguably the "father" of the modern West Highland White Terrier) wrote for Rawdon Lee's *Modern Dog* in 1894, "They are gameness itself, and terrible poachers. They love above all things to get away with a young retriever, and ruin him forever, teaching him everything he ought not to know." These feisty white terriers were bred to hunt vermin and small predators; in fact, Edward Malcolm's Westies virtually wiped out the fox population around his estate in the 1890s.

Today, for the most part, the West Highland White Terrier remains in the hands of capable stewards. The changes to the original breed have been minor: The shortening of the back is perhaps a small compromise that doesn't seem to have affected the Westie's natural talents and prowess for hunting.

THE WESTIE MYSTIQUE: LOOKS, BRAINS, AND MAKEUP

Alert-looking, adorable, and stylish, Westies are functional little dogs with an attractive balance of soundness and athleticism, making them ready for just about anything. They're 110 percent terrier, crammed full of Scottish hardiness, moxie, and a large measure of temerity, tenacity, and loyalty. It's truly incredible that so much can be distilled into such a small package. Westies love the outdoors; they are excellent hunters with efficient little bodies and a canniness that amuses and amazes. They also love their homes, and are happy to curl up contentedly by the hearth, safely out of the blustery cold.

The "package" of the West Highland White Terrier is small but potent. One of the relatively short-legged terriers indigenous to the rocky, rough contour of the Scottish terrain, he has the substance and strength needed to deal with those challenging lands. The Westie has strong front legs, thick nails and pads, with an ever-so-slight turnout to the front feet—which are larger that the rear ones. This trait is essential so that he can move the earth sideways in search of his quarry without the risk of digging himself into his hole.

The Westie possesses strong jaws, large teeth, and keen intelligence, as well as the high predatory drive appropriate to his life's work. This is a dog that's changed little since his beginnings and, at best, whose "form follows his function." The changes effected by selective breeding have been few—the most notable being a slight increase in substance and a slight shortening of the back, which does not appear to alter function. The bigger changes have been more superficial (grooming styles among them). Westies have been tidied up for exhibition in dog shows, something exhibitors have found necessary for competing in the cutthroat Terrier Group ring—with its highly stylized and meticulously groomed competitors, with their tighter-plucked jackets and manicured look—as well as in the Best in Show ring.

Composed for the benefit of dog show exhibitors, the breed standard describes the quintessential Westie—a written vision of the ideal. While perfection does not exist in the dog world (or anywhere on earth, for that matter), for a Westie to become a show dog, he should fit the standard's specifications as closely as possible. Breeders strive to produce dogs that "conform" to the official breed standard, hence the word *conformation*—meaning a dog show.

General Appearance

Small but confident, plucky and hardy, the West Highland White Terrier is a beautifully balanced, stellar showman of a dog possessing a deep chest and well-sprung ribs. His back is straight and level and his hindquarters strong. He's an agile, active, and efficient mover with a seemingly endless reserve of endurance. His double coat is composed of a topcoat of hard guard hairs—which should ideally be about two inches (5 cm) long—and a downy thermal protective undercoat. When groomed for show, the coat is neatened up—leaving more hair on the back and sides but blended into a shorter neck and shoulder coat. Longer hair is left to frame the face to reveal the typical smart Westie.

Size, Proportion, and Substance

The breed standard for the Westie states that 11 inches (27.9 cm) at the withers for males and 10 inches (25.4 cm) for females is most desirable, but some variation, within

The Westie's head should be groomed to a round appearance and should be in good proportion to the body.

reason, is accepted. More important is the impression of a compact dog with good balance and substance—and moderation.

Head

The Westie's head should be groomed to a round appearance and should be in good proportion to the body. The broad, substantial, slightly domed skull underneath the hair ought to be a bit longer than his muzzle, gradually tapering to the eyes. A blunt muzzle with powerful jaws tapers to the nose, which should be large and black as licorice; so should the lips.

A Westie's teeth are his stock-in-trade, and the bigger the teeth, the better. Six incisors must be present on both the upper and lower jaws between the canines. A snug scissors bite or a level bite is acceptable, but an overshot or and undershot mouth or one with misaligned, missing incisors or several missing premolars is severely faulted.

Winter Nose

During times of limited sunshine, winter nose or "snow nose" may occur, in which the Westie's nose loses some of its black pigment. Calcium and vitamin D (and, of course, sunshine) can correct this temporary and harmless condition, which generally rights itself as the days grow longer.

Expression

"Wonderfully inquisitive and alert" describes the Westie's expression. Wide set, slightly sunken eyes edged by black kohl-like pigmentation present a striking appearance. Eyes should be of almond shape, dark brown, and intelligent looking. Heavy eyebrows enhance the piercing look.

Ears

Ears should be small, pricked, and carried erect, widely set, and ending in a sharp tip. Short trimming leaves ears smooth and velvety with no errant hairs at the tips. Dark pigmentation on the skin at the ears' tips is desirable.

The Westie's expression should be inquisitive and alert; intelligent-looking dark brown eyes are also desired.

Neck, Topline, and Body

The Westie should be well muscled, well set on sloping shoulders, and his length should be in good proportion to the rest of his body. Medium is key here—the neck ought not be either too long or too short. A Westie's body should be compact—but again, not too short—and substantial without being coarse. Ribs should be deep, well sprung, and heart shaped. The chest should be deep and should extend to the elbows in good proportion.

His carrot-shaped tail should be carried as straight as possible and not curled over the back; its length should not exceed the top of the skull. Undocked and covered with hard hair, it should be set straight on at back level.

Angulation and Shoulders

Shoulder blades should be well laid back and connected at the spine, attaching to a moderately long upper arm, which allows the body to overhang. A faulty shoulder is one that is too straight, too steep, or one with too short an upper arm. This type of assembly impedes the Westie's movement.

Legs

Front legs should be straight, muscular, covered with short, hard hair, and set directly under the shoulders. The lengths from the withers to the elbow and the elbow to the ground should be nearly equal.

Feet

For a Westie, large, round forefeet—larger than the hind feet—are correct and desirable. Ideally, feet should have thick black pads and nails, and there should be a slight turnout at the foot—on otherwise nice, straight legs.

Hindquarters

Muscular, well-angulated thighs should not be set wide apart. Hocks should be well bent and should look parallel from the rear. Hind legs should be fairly short, with strong hocks. Hind feet should be smaller than forefeet, and thick black pads are most desirable.

Gait

A Westie should move freely, easily, and straight—with a definite reach and drive. This is a double-tracking terrier. *Double tracking* refers to the movement of a dog when he reaches forward; in Westies the front-paw movement is fairly parallel, so that each paw makes a separate track, in contrast to most breeds, whose front feet converge toward a single point, or track. Still, double-tracking terriers such as Westies tend to move toward the center of gravity.

Rear movement is ideally free and strong, with the hocks freely flexing and drawing close under the body, so the dog

Too Muscular?

A "loaded shoulder," considered a fault in the Westie, occurs when the shoulder blades are shoved out from the body by overdeveloped muscles. Westies should not have a Superman physique.

can propel itself with adequate force. This is an efficient-moving dog, built for stamina. Flexibility and agility is essential for maneuvering the terrain of its country of origin.

Coat

The Westie's coat is one of his most important assets. A double coat is a must. The outer coat should consist of hard, straight, white hair, of approximately 2 inches (5 cm) in length. The coat is best stripped shorter on the neck and shoulders, and blended smoothly into the longer furnishings of the head, jacket, and skirt—which remain long. The harder, the straighter, the whiter the outer coat is, the more desirable. A bit of wheaten tipping on a hard, straight coat is considered more correct than a fluffy pure white coat. (In dogs, "wheaten" is a pale, yellowish to ruddy fawn color.) Furnishings can be softer than the main jacket, but they should never appear fluffy. Soft coats, single coats, dead coats, blown coats, and short coats are all a no-no.

Color

White! It's actually a part of the breed's name: West Highland *White* Terrier. There is a range of whiteness here, but any coat color other than white, such as a heavy wheaten color, is penalized in competition.

Some breeders think color and harshness of the coat are related. Sandy Davis of Lanarkstone Kennels has observed over her many years of breeding that soft coats are often whiter, but there are always exceptions to this. Although a harsher coat often accompanies a darker shade, these traits

The Westie's Functional Coat

The Westie's double coat is fully functional. The topcoat of hard guard hairs repels water, and his downy, soft undercoat insulates him from the frequently inclement weather of his place of origin—the Scottish moors and highlands. It also provides natural defense against the nasty adversaries that challenge him—particularly in his indigenous terrain—like fierce animals and unforgiving prickly bramble. The undercoat naturally grows thicker around the neck area to protect against injury and attacks.

Show grooming used to require at least two inches of healthy coat. Now, tighter, tidier grooming with a much more manicured look is favored over the more casual, natural style that used to be favored. This change came about in an effort to make Westies more competitive against the more stylized terriers in the group.

The Westie has a double coat that is fully functional—it repels water and keeps him warm.

are determined by two separate genes. A darker coat shade seems related to a genetically occurring "dorsal streak," which can be exacerbated by the dryness of a particularly coarse coat. This is why you tend to see this streak in harsh-coated dogs most often. Dorsal streaks run along the top of the back and upper sides of the body, but are absent from the head, legs, lower body, front, and sides of the neck. This trait, though not universal, is not uncommon. Naturally, most breeders and judges do not want to see a dorsal streak, although the breed standard was changed in 1988 to reflect the fact that dogs may have slight color in the coat. Still, it's the whiter dogs that are preferred in the show ring. But of course, breeders strive for the best of both worlds: a nice harsh coat in a bright, vibrant "angel wing" white!

The skin of the Westie should ideally have a gray tinge. A gray-pink color on the skin and dark gray ear points are desired, accompanied by black eye and lip rims, although many Westies have pink skin.

White Dog Problems

Westie breeders have strived toward the whitest coats possible, but taking this too far has the potential to encourage problems such as those seen in some of the "true" white dogs—Bull Terriers, white Boxers, and other such breeds. These breeds commonly show a tendency toward deafness and blindness. Though these problems are uncommon in Westies, John T. Marvin, long considered an authority on the breed, admonishes breeders to be aware of the link between the depth of pigmentation and its effect on Westie well-being. It is equally important for the buyer to be wary. When choosing a puppy, look for dark pigmentation on the pads. That decreases your risk of "white dog problems." (Thick, dark pads also indicate that the dog has the toughness that developed in the breed as a necessity of navigating their rough, indigenous terrain.)

Most important, though, is the foundation of the West Highland White Terrier as a functional, healthy, strong terrier. Structure is too often sacrificed for that pure white coat. Breeder Dee Hanna asks—rhetorically, one hopes, "Would you eat a strychnine cake if it were frosted with the whitest, most beautiful and tasty frosting in the world?"

Temperament

This little terrier is ready for anything. He's bold but not belligerent; if confronted, he's not about to turn tail and run away. He's feisty, intelligent, extremely adept at problem solving, and moderately obedient. He's more responsive to obedience training than many other breeds. Terriers are not known for being "pleaser" dogs, but Westies can be the exception. Bargains between Westies and their handlers have

Is the Westie Really a White Dog?

Yes and no. Westies are actually "off-white" or yellow dogs with modifying factors in their genetic makeup that make them appear white. This explains the dark pigment on their pads, noses, lips, and eye rims. The whiteness is nuanced—almost like the different interior "white" wall paints you'll likely find at your local hardware store. Westies can have coat colors that contain variations of white, blue white, cream white, and so on. "There have got to be about twenty-five shades of white in the Westie," longtime breeder and professional handler, Dee Hanna (D and D Kennels) comments. Check an interior wall-paint chart, or swatches of bridal-gown fabrics in eggshell or ivory to see the enormous range of whites. Or imagine descriptions of Westie colors like "glacier," "snowdrop," "lily of the valley," "vanilla ice," "silver lined," "cloudburst," "meringue," and you should get the picture.

been struck many times, and they can be trained and have wowed more than one judge or show spectator.

Despite their independence, many Westies have excelled in the obedience ring. Most Westie owners who compete in obedience competitions acquire their dogs because they love the breed's personality—obedience is merely an afterthought. Westies are among the most people oriented of the terrier group, and they generally do not hold grudges. Inquisitive, upbeat, and persistent, they do like to please— and it's a double bonus for them to please themselves as well as their owners. Although the self-reliance and independent hunting ability they were bred for can sometimes be an obstacle, those traits are not certain deterrents to obedience. The standard is quite clear in stating that Westies must be neither timid nor pugnacious.

IS THE WESTIE YOUR DREAM DOG?

Before deciding to bring home a Westie, the first question you need to ask yourself is, "Why do I want a dog?" Owning a dog will not save a relationship; it will not help an uncooperative child learn responsibility. The dog may be great "date bait," but the success of your relationship will not ultimately rest on your Westie's lily-white shoulders. If you are thinking of adopting a Westie for your child (and Westies aren't the best choice for children under the age of six), realize that you will end up as his prime caretaker. If your child becomes involved, that's gravy, but you can't expect it. A responsible breeder will look for signs that the adult is at least as excited—or more excited—by the prospect of inviting a Westie to join the family.

If you choose well, you'll get a wonderful, intelligent companion with a good sense of humor, and a pal who is game for almost anything this side of bungee jumping. The West Highland White Terrier Club of America has a questionnaire called "The Westie Profiler" on its website, www.westieclubamerica.com, which offers some insight on the question, "Is a West Highland White Terrier the right dog for you?" It's a great tool for deciding if the Westie is your dream dog.

ARE YOU A WESTIE'S DREAM MATE?

The key is adaptability. A West Highland White Terrier

Telepathic Westies?

O'Raigan Kennels' Mary Lou Ludlow, a breeder in Oregon for nearly forty years, insists that her Westies are telepathic. "Sure, they can be stubborn," she admits. And they can outplay, outwit, and outlast practically anything or anybody. But she insists that nonverbal communication invariably achieves the desired result when she wills her Westie companion, Jackie-O, to come when she mentally "calls."

If you live in the country, you'll want to keep an eye on your Westie, even if he is in an enclosed area.

can thrive almost anywhere there's someone to love him and keep him secure. But how adaptable are you?

Time Needs

Do you have enough time to spend with your Westie? It's necessary to be available for the dog for frequent companionship; a bored and lonely Westie can act out destructively—even if he doesn't see it that way. Even the best-cared-for West Highland White Terrier may act out because of his instinctual desire to hunt rodents. Balance between work and love works best for a happy Westie, so he should not be kept in solitary confinement. He likes his space, but he also loves his owner—not in an obnoxious or obsequious way—and he's loyal to the end. When he wants to be with you, you will know it.

Independence

It has been said that he "won't take no for an answer." No, he figures, is a mere consideration—a temporary barrier to yes. Although a good alpha human is necessary so that your Westie doesn't abscond with your credit cards and tell you how to use them, control freaks and Westies don't mesh well.

As much as they like to please their loved ones, they also cherish their independence and practice a degree of free will. A puppy socialization class that teaches general manners will enhance your relationship. The curriculum may not specifically address this aspect of the Westie persona, but a competent and observant instructor should help you establish who's boss.

City Slicker, Suburban Sentinel, or Thank-God-I'm-a-Country-Dog?

West Highland White Terriers are an adaptable breed. Some living situations may seem more desirable than others, but if a Westie's owners have the sufficient dedication and commitment, the dog can thrive in practically every environment. Some situations may, however, require adjustments—and plenty of tender loving care. Breeder Sandy Davis of Lanarkstone Kennels feels that a Westie deserves a home where he is loved and considered a member of the family, and where there is a lifetime commitment to him. Davis has visions of an "ideal home" (i.e., someone home all day, fenced yard, and so on) but has successfully placed Westies in homes where the physical reality was different from that ideal. Flexibility is never a bad thing.

In the City

As long as you exercise him frequently and allow him to explore the world—on leash, of course—Westies can be very amenable to life in the metropolis. Obey laws to curb your dog and be sure and pick up all waste. From the Westie's point of view, the city is a feast for the nose. "Pee-mail" from other dogs will alert him to a tremendous underground canine community. Take advantage of parks and green spots. But keep in mind that even cities aren't immune to predators. In the Detroit Metro area, Westie owners have reported stories of foxes preying on small dogs. Owls, hawks, and eagles may also appear overhead in many cities.

In the Suburbs

Westies make perfect suburban watchdogs; they're living, breathing security systems. Their formidable bark belies their size. In fact, your doorbell could become obsolete. First-class deterrents for would-be burglars, Westies will

As long as you provide him with plenty of exercise, your Westie can get by happily in an apartment setting.

alert residents and neighbors of any suspicious behavior. They are your "neighborhood-watch" dogs. However, most are pretty sorry excuses for guard dogs.

A fenced yard on the order of a stockade is necessary, as these terriers are master diggers—in some cases, veritable miniature backhoes wearing white uniforms. Remember that these are clever, problem-solving dogs with Houdini-like escape abilities.

Keep your Westie on a leash when you are out and about. Even the best-trained terriers may only be 99 percent reliable: That one squirrel or critter darting across a busy street can claim that 1 percent and cause more grief than you can bear. Westies have a prey drive that rivals the best.

In the Country

In the country, you'll want to keep an eye on him, even if he's confined to a fenced area. Birds of prey, coyotes, cougars, and other wildlife could threaten your Westie. Never let him out after dark—even if he's confined (as he should be).

But your Westie can also be useful, as Westies have always been, at keeping the rodent, mole, and gopher population in check. Right now, somewhere in the world, a pack of West Highland White Terriers is playing tug-of-war with a possum. Some will eat a bit of what they catch, in essence living off the fat of the land. Many will roll around in really odiferous substances. Others enjoy their fruits and vegetables, and are adept at picking blueberries and other toothsome treats.

Age and Longevity

In general, Westies are long-lived, but that, of course, is never long enough. You can generally expect to have your companion with you for at least 12 to 16 years—and some will remain with you for even longer—sometimes up to 18 or 20 years.

Exercise Needs

A West Highlander will gratefully take whatever exercise he can. He loves to run, play, and tussle. Many are ball players, retrievers, flyballers, and some are making quite a name for themselves in competitive obedience and agility. Certain Westies and their "partners" enjoy freestyle obedience, sometimes referred to as "dancing with your dog." But it's far more than that—although the result can look like something out of an old Fred Astaire and Ginger Rogers movie (except that neither you nor your dog are required to do it in high heels, backwards).

Most Westies adore the thrill of the chase. And since their conformation has changed so little, they remain among the truly functional terriers. They love to go on hikes—especially to places where the terrain is rough and challenging. They move across and around obstacles with confidence and stamina.

Exercise is essential to keep them in good shape. Westies are capable of creating their own games and exercise regimes along with the ones they play with you, so a fenced yard and/or an owner who is willing to take reasonably long walks is beneficial. Suffice it to say that the marvelous things you can do with your Westie are numerous.

Westie Tale: The City

Laurie Cochin's family, which includes her Westie, Sally, lives in an apartment on the Upper East Side of Manhattan. Sally loves to sit outside and watch the world go by while Laurie chats with all her doggy friends on their busy New York City street. Laurie reports, "One night, on her last walk of the day, she just rolled on her side and fell fast asleep on the sidewalk! People actually pointed to her and said, 'By the way, do you know your dog is asleep?' I had no idea. . ."

Competing in agility is a great way to exercise your Westie.

Other Pets

Some believe that Westies are more placid than other terriers—milder. But Westies will react if they perceive that they're put upon. An adaptable breed, Westies can be happy as "only dogs" or can enjoy living with other dogs. But they do like attention.

Westies—especially ones that have been spayed or neutered—can be highly compatible with other animals. If you have two, your optimal couple would be one of each sex. Two neutered males can work well, although two intact males can be trouble (and quadruple trouble if there's a fertile female in the equation). Keeping two females, spayed or intact, can be tricky. They may decide they like each other, but heaven help you if they don't. Two bitches hell-bent on eliminating each other can be very unpleasant and costly in terms of vet bills if you do not separate them.

As for feline friendships, variables exist. Westies and cats can be the best of friends: This is especially true if you bring a young puppy into a household where the cat already resides. But if your Westie predates the cat, you might find the cat poring over the classifieds in search of new digs . . .

In general, Westies don't tend to form deep friendships with rats, guinea pigs, or ferrets. These creatures risk losing not only their turf but also their lives!

Westies and Children

This can be a beautiful combination—like root beer and ice cream—but the best relationships are forged with care and respect for both the Westie and the child. Sadly, puppies are at great risk when in contact with unthinking or overly exuberant children. On the other hand, some recent studies have shown that early childhood exposure to pets reduces the chances of children developing allergies—and not just to pets.

Many breeders are careful to find a situation where children are older—at least six or seven—well supervised, and where they will be taught how to treat their potential playmate with respect. Success depends upon the degree of supervision of both dog and child—again, it is essential for the adult to teach the child proper respect for the puppy's rights. Although complete responsibility for a Westie's care and feeding should never rest on the shoulders of a child, adults can do much to teach children basic care and to set reasonable limits that will take into account both the dog's and the child's rights.

Older, well-socialized children can have a blast with their Westies. Many Westies are quite athletic; they may love to retrieve tennis balls, to play catch, or to act like canine Pelés when it comes to soccer. Certain Westies have demonstrated sophisticated footwork; since they never have to worry about getting their hands on the ball, Westies have a great advantage over their human opponents. Some will even execute "headers" that rival those observed in World Cup tournaments!

However, rough children of any age are a liability to Westies; parents should exercise great vigilance to make sure a child never gets too aggressive—and if the child does, supervision must be increased to prevent injury to either the dog or the child. In general, a Westie is not the best choice for a neighborhood where scads of kids congregate to play.

Did You Know?

The two dogs used on the bottle of Black and White Scotch were the Scottish Terrier and the West Highland White. The dogs on the bottle were named "Blackie" and "Whitey." Many people have erroneously assumed that "Whitey" was a "melanin-challenged" Scottie. False!

All the excitement and activity are almost irresistible to your Westie's prey drive. The stimulation may be just too much for him and could result in nonmalicious—but nevertheless dangerous—nipping. These are tough little dogs, and with excessive action and motion they have the potential to act like athletes on steroids.

Westies can get along well with children as long as proper respect is taught.

If a Baby Arrives

Though breeders don't recommend Westies to families with newborn babies or toddlers, sometimes the pair is inevitable—especially if the Westie was there first. The arrival of a new baby is cause for stepped-up, "Code Orange" security. It can be a bit easier to teach your dog the new rules before the baby is ambulatory. You can introduce the dog to the baby and its smells from a distance, but you certainly don't want to place the two in the same playpen just because it would make a cute photo. And please *don't leave them alone together for one moment.*

As the baby grows, the various stages of development offer opportunities to teach the baby how to treat the dog properly. Toys can become veritable "bones of contention," so it's best not to allow the baby and the dog to sit among the baby's toys—or the baby to sit among the dog's playthings. In such situations, your Westie may consider the baby equivalent to a littermate and vie for dominance. (There are also sanitary reasons.)

Eventually, you can teach the baby to pet the dog gently—without squeezing—to leave him alone while he's in his crate, and to never disturb the dog while he's eating (disturbing him is asking for trouble). It is also important to teach the baby never to hit the dog, hassle him, scream at him, or drag him around. Training a child to treat a pet well offers an opportunity to establish the importance of boundaries and respect—relevant in any relationship. So what might not appear to be an optimum situation can be turned into an opportunity if handled with watchfulness and understanding. Westie and baby will grow up together, and with a foundation of mutual respect, the growing child may naturally wish to take on some of the responsibilities of caring for the dog. Picking up the dog's toys (assuming that you haven't already taught your Westie to pick up his own toys—as well as your child's), accompanying you and the dog to the vet, and helping you prepare the dog's meal can help cement a bond between your two cherished ones.

Teaching Table Manners

Make it very clear to your children—and it is often necessary to repeat this to yourself and to any other adults in the family—that no one is to feed the Westie from the table. It's tempting for little Ashley to pawn off her generous portion of unwanted haggis to the dog, who considers it as good as—well—haggis (he is Scottish, after all). If you don't enforce this rule, you'll end up with a pudgy little dog with an annoying habit of disrupting meals on a regular basis.

PREPARING
FOR YOUR WEST HIGHLAND WHITE TERRIER

Sure, he may appear white as the driven snow, but he's 100 percent terrier—attractive and stylish on the outside, but tough on the inside. Capable of convincing lenient owners to let him get away with mischief, he's a giant dog compressed into a small body. He may sometimes even act like the angel he resembles, but there's a bit of the devil in him too. Nevertheless, this sweet, lovable terrier is ever ready for work or play, and his individual personality is every bit as unique as the human with whom he shares his home.

PUPPY OR ADULT?

Some people have never considered that they may have a choice between a young puppy and an older Westie. To avoid the difficulty of and the necessary vigilance that comes with adding a puppy to your family, getting an older puppy or even a mature dog may be just the ticket. In some cases, an older Westie may already be housebroken and crate trained, or simply better suited to your living situation.

A Westie Puppy

Many people prefer a puppy because they think he will be veritable "putty in their hands," able to be molded to fit their needs. This thinking is only partly correct. There are personality traits, characteristics, and genetic propensities hardwired into the breed. Once you've determined that you're up to the demands of a tenacious terrier—sometimes with his own agenda—then you can work within those parameters and try to educate or "lead out" your puppy to adapt to your requirements. But it is hard work to socialize a creature with such great temerity, strong instincts—and hypodermic needle-sharp teeth. You will have the opportunity to set the boundaries, and with the feisty Westie, it will be an adventure and an exercise in patience—guaranteed!

Remember that although a Westie puppy is irresistible beyond belief, taking on your young charge is no small commitment. Housetraining, bite inhibition (which one hopes the breeder has at least initiated), and keeping tabs on the puppy when he's not confined to a crate can be a 24/7 job. Some Westies are veritable garbage disposals and will chew or ingest anything not nailed down.

One of your first decisions will be whether a Westie puppy or adult is right for you.

A Westie Adult

Many hobby breeders will place a retired champion, stud dog, or brood bitch to make room in their breeding programs for newer stock. Or, a breeder will keep a show prospect, only later to decide to place the dog in a pet home. These dogs are in good health (or any health issues will be identified) and deserve good homes. Also, breeders generally charge less for them. You can also find Westie adults through rescues, and occasionally shelters.

A well-socialized Westie with a stable temperament will adapt beautifully to a new, loving home. He will probably be thrilled to become the center of attention in his new home. He may be housebroken and have had some basic training, and as long as he's loved and cherished and treated with patience and consistency, you'll win his heart. Find out all you can about his past—history, habits, likes, pet peeves, and diet. If well treated and loved, he will never look back, he'll only look forward to his life with his new family.

Many breeders suggest a trial period to ensure a good match. If your dog's primary caretaker can initially take some time off to help him adjust to his new environment, it's a boon. After about a month, consider an obedience class. Not only will it teach him skills or reinforce ones he already has, it will cement the bond between the two of you.

WESTIE LADDIE OR WESTIE LASSIE?

Which make better pets, males or females? Both are great—but if you're adding a puppy, and your preexisting dog is a male, the best choice for a second dog is a female (especially if one or both are or will be spayed or neutered). Two neutered males are the next-best option, but adding a second bitch can be dicey. Two females can get along, but for some, it's "hate at first sight," and they will make each other—and you—miserable. There are many exceptions, but why tempt fate?

Males are perfect for people who want a "giving" pet. If you prefer to "care for" a pet, choose a female. If you ask most breeders, they'll agree that the males are generally more affectionate than the females, who tend toward independence. But both make great pets, and you should choose the individual dog with whom you relate best. Many breeders excel at matching puppy to potential owner. But regardless of gender, most dogs grow up to be a combination of their genetic makeup and exactly what their owners train them to be.

WHERE TO FIND THE WESTIE OF YOUR DREAMS

Once you've made the decision that the Westie is the breed for you, it's time to explore your options on where to buy, rescue, or adopt your new best friend.

Breeder

By far, the best choice of breeder is the so-called "hobby breeder," despite the somewhat misleading name. This person breeds for sheer love of the breed, not for profit. In fact, she probably spends more money breeding, showing, testing, and caring for her Westies than she earns from selling the occasional pet. In her quest for improving the breed and producing the best Westies she can, she exhibits her dogs at shows to gauge how close she can come to breeding the "ideal Westie." This kind of breeder enjoys the respect she has earned among other breeders and will be as careful and honest in selling you a pet as she is in placing her show dogs. Membership in the local Westie or WHTCA indicates that a

When visiting a breeder, look over the puppies to see if they are healthy.

breeder networks with others currently in the breed and presumably breeds according to a prescribed code of ethics.

Locating a Good Breeder

Most responsible hobby breeders do not advertise. So how do you find one? The secretary or breeder referral person of your local Westie club or all-breed club may be able to direct you to a member who is planning a litter or who might have a dog available. If you're online, the AKC website can direct you to a Westie breeder near you.

Dog shows are among the best places to locate a good hobby breeder. Shows are where you'll see what a Westie should look like, and you may get a chance to speak to breeders. If you see a Westie that particularly strikes your fancy, ask the handler if he knows of anyone who is expecting a litter related to this dog. Some people are a little tense before exhibiting their dogs, so wait until breed judging has ended before approaching the handler.

Most breeders love educating those curious about their breed, but should you encounter someone who is rude, don't take it personally. Perhaps she just lost in the ring, so she takes it out on the nearest target—you. Keeping trying, and talk to someone else.

Show Quality Versus Pet Quality

Some breeders will offer both "show quality" and "pet quality" Westies. Of course when it comes to quality, it's impossible for anyone to ascertain whether a young puppy will work out as a show dog. The breeder simply hedges her bets. Many "keepers" have had their bite reverse or a testicle stay lodged in the abdomen, while a "less-than-perfect prospect" morphs into a knockout, causing at least one breeder to kick herself for letting him go. But no one really loses in the end. Both "show quality" and "pet quality" dogs should be healthy and of wonderful temperament.

Visiting the Breeder

When you visit the breeder, you can see the whole litter with their dam. If the sire isn't present, ask to see a photo. Caring breeders are very particular about the homes their puppies go to, so expect an interrogation. They may want to know what kinds of dogs you've had in the past and how long the dog will be left alone each day; some ask to check out your house and yard. This may seem intrusive, but all you have to gain is a happy, healthy, well-socialized Westie puppy from a breeder who cares—and an ally!

At the breeder's, the puppies' environment should be kept clean, and the puppies should appear bright-eyed, healthy, and playful with their littermates. Observe how they interact with humans as well. Young Westie puppies should not live exclusively in outdoor kennels, nor should they be confined to a shed or flimsy outbuilding. Home-raised puppies stand the best chance of becoming ideal pets.

Co-ownership

The breeder may offer to "co-own" a show-quality dog with you, so that the dog may obtain his AKC Championship. If the Westie is a female, the breeder may want to whelp a litter. In most cases, this means the breeder makes the arrangements to show her, while you can still keep her as a pet most of the time. All this should be clearly indicated in the contract. If you want to learn to show and groom your Westie, some breeders make outstanding mentors. However, co-ownerships have their risks, and the concept attracts its share of control freaks, so proceed cautiously.

Questions to Ask the Breeder

Don't be afraid to ask the breeder questions, either. If anything, the breeder will be impressed that you have done your research. Ask her how she got started breeding and showing. Willingness to share enthusiasm is a hallmark of a good breeder. How long has she been breeding Westies? (More than three years is good if this is your first Westie.) What can the breeder tell you about your puppy's ancestors? Trust your intuition and don't be impulsive. Take your time and ask away!

An ethical breeder will be honest about the pros and cons of owning a Westie. She should be familiar with the breed's most common health issues. If she denies ever having had any health problems, she is either being dishonest or she hasn't been in the breed very long. Also, be very suspicious of breeders who whelp one litter after another.

Request references from previous customers, follow up, and ask them questions about the Westie they bought from this breeder. A breeder who balks at this or tries to minimize the opinions of their other clients may not be your best bet. Also, most devoted Westie breeders will ask that the pup be returned to them if for any reason you decide you need to give it up.

Temperament Tests

Some good breeders use temperament tests to assist them in evaluating the behavioral tendencies of a pup. Breeders use them for the following reasons:
- to help select puppies for show or obedience.
- to place puppies in the most appropriate homes.
- to determine how to encourage the puppies to grow into mentally sound adults.

This test is fairly reliable and points to character tendencies. Remember that environment also plays a great role in shaping temperament; nevertheless, temperament testing can be a valuable tool for placing a puppy in his best environment.

Backyard Breeder

You need to be wary of certain breeders, often called "backyard breeders." This type of breeder is not always malevolent, but they can often be unaware of important

Ask the breeder plenty of questions—he or she should happily answer you.

genetic and health issues that good breeders watch out for. If you choose to buy from one of these breeders, you should subject him to the same degree of questioning that you should any breeder. However, run like the wind if any of the following are true of the breeder:

- He makes his living from selling dogs. He typically has a number of breeds, sometimes as many as ten to twenty—and offers puppies of each.
- She doesn't ask many questions and doesn't want to answer many either.
- He doesn't test the dogs for genetic problems.
- Price comes up early in the conversation (usually first).
- She will sell to anyone—no questions asked.
- He refuses to show you the facility where the dogs are housed.
- She arranges to meet you in a parking lot of a factory outlet mall to sell you your puppy.

Rescue Me!

West Highland White Terrier Rescue can be an excellent source for acquiring an older dog (rescues rarely have

Registering Your Dog

American Kennel Club (AKC)

When you buy a dog represented as AKC eligible, the seller should give you a properly filled out AKC Dog Registration Application form. Submitting the completed form with the fee enables you to register the dog with AKC. After processing is complete, you receive an AKC Registration Certificate. Sometimes a breeder will sell you a dog on a Limited Registration. This is to encourage you to sterilize the dog. Offspring of dogs registered on a Limited Registration will not be AKC eligible. A Limited Registration entitles your dog to participate in all AKC activities except conformation.

The Kennel Club

At the time of the sale, the breeder will sign and date the Breeder Registration Certificate, which the new owner will receive with the puppy and all other documentation. The new owner completes a Change of Ownership form by supplying the required information on the back and returns it to the Kennel Club within ten days for the Kennel Club to validate.

The new owner receives Kennel Club Registration Documents, a full color Registration Certificate, and a booklet that provides general information about the Kennel Club and the fascinating world of purebred dogs in England.

puppies). Not only can you find a wonderful companion, you can help a dog in need. A grateful Westie is a wellspring of affection to the human who gives him the love and attention he deserves. Please note that some rescued dogs come with health and behavioral issues that need to be addressed, although often these issues ease or disappear with the work of dedicated foster homes, generous advice from experts, and consistent follow-up in the adoptive home.

Where do these rescued Westies come from? Some may have been rescued from puppy mills, but most are surrendered because of extenuating circumstances, such as the death of an owner, difficulties with young children, or residential restrictions. Others come from households that were just not prepared to care for a dog.

The key is finding a rescue organization that understands the crucial importance of balancing these dogs' needs with those of the people who adopt them. A club like the West Highland White Terrier Club of Southeastern Michigan (WHWTCSEM) has implemented the policy of not placing any rescue Westies in households with children younger than ten. Policies differ slightly among the various regional groups, but Beth Widdows, WHWTCSEM Club Rescue chair, finds that her club's policy promotes higher success rates.

Westie rescue organizations affiliated with the national club have strict codes of conduct and require that rescue applicants undergo thorough screening. These groups never knowingly place dogs with biting issues or major aggression issues. Sadly, the people who surrender them sometimes consider rescue organizations (and shelters) "dumping grounds" for a maladjusted, aggressive dog (often that way through the family's own fault) that they were ill equipped to nurture in the first place. For this reason, assuming they have resources, most rescues try to foster their dogs before placement.

Not only can rescuing a Westie provide you with an excellent companion, it can mean helping a dog in need.

Rescue Westies, some of unknown background and others who carry more emotional baggage than those with happier beginnings, can potentially bring with them handsome rewards. Plus, with their devotion, they remind you that you can make a difference in an innocent animal's life. But more than likely, you'll end up feeling gratitude toward them for letting *you* into their lives. You can find a Westie rescue through www.westieclubamerica.com/rescue/.

Rescue Success Stories

Maggie Mae, adopted from Westie Rescue of Missouri became WHWTCA's Versatile Dog Maggie Mae Beason, CGC, TDI, CG, CD, ME. She came to rescue unsprayed and with a large hernia. After her convalescence, volunteers transported her to Illinois, where she lives with her Westie "brother," Winston, and her human, Pam Groves. She is the first rescue Westie ever to have earned a prestigious Versatility Award.

Rescue dog Maggie Mae.

Portraits of rescue dog Glennie and his "sister," Molly.

Glendennin's Pride, CGC, NAP, NJP, was abandoned at seven months of age and adopted by his foster "mother." Glennie's issues included fear of men and separation anxiety. Helped by many, including a male truck driver/rescue volunteer and then a dedicated male instructor, he overcame his fears. Now more confident than ever, Glennie earned his Canine Good Citizen and began agility training (and has earned his novice titles), earthdog, and obedience. He lives with his Westie sister, Molly, and has become a happy little boy.

Gimme Shelter

Occasionally a Westie will come into a shelter, but they are hard to come by—and the paucity of smaller dogs means that, if they're adoptable, they're likely to be snatched up quickly. But it doesn't hurt to check, or you can search www.petfinder.org.

Pet Stores

Some people decide to buy their Westie from a pet store. Pet stores can be a convenient option, and many offer a wide selection of puppies. The dogs in a pet store are most often well cared for by the staff—fed nutritious food, provided with toys, and kept clean. It's hard to resist them, especially when the store employee offers to let you play with those tiny little guys. It is important to remember that a dog's health is largely dependent on his genetics and the quality of his early care. This is why a responsible pet store should be able to provide you with all the details of your Westie's breeding and history. Pet store employees should also be knowledgeable about dogs in general and the breeds they sell in particular.

If you decide to purchase a Westie from a pet store, check

the dog for any signs of poor health. A few signs of illness are nasal discharge, watery eyes, and diarrhea. A store should not be selling a dog experiencing any of these symptoms. Even if the puppy seems healthy, be sure to have him checked by your veterinarian as soon as possible. Many health guarantees offered by pet stores are contingent upon a veterinary examination within just days of the sale.

Questions to Ask Before Purchasing a Pet Store Puppy

1. *What kind of guarantee do you offer?*

If the store only guarantees the puppy for a few hours or days but offers no compensation for future problems such as genetic diseases, you must be aware that you will be on your own to deal with these problems. The store should be reasonably responsible for ensuring you receive a healthy puppy.

2. *How old was the puppy when he arrived in the store?*

Puppies taken away from their mother and littermates before eight weeks of age are at a great developmental disadvantage. Puppies learn a lot about social interaction from their mother and littermates, and getting shipped across the country in a crate is no way to begin life as a six-week-old puppy. Those taken away too young and exposed to these frightening experiences often develop fearful or aggressive behaviors later in life. The best-case scenario is one in which the puppy was hand delivered by a breeder to a pet store after eight weeks of age.

3. *Can I see the vaccination and worming record?*

Puppies should have had at least one and preferably two sets of complete vaccinations and a worming by eight weeks (this can also depend on the breed). The pet store should have complete documentation of these and any other veterinary care the dogs have received.

4. *Is the puppy registered?*

This is actually a tricky question. Registration is no guarantee of quality, and some registries will register any dog without proof of a pedigree (a written record of a dog's lineage). Dogs who are registered with the American Kennel Club (AKC) or Kennel Club (KC) may be more likely to come from breeders who are following certain standards, but it's not a guarantee. And some small local breeders may provide puppies to pet stores

Did You Know?

Show breeders often keep only one or two puppies for show and sell the rest as "pets." Often the differences are subtle. These pets have been bred with the same health, temperament, and looks as the future champions.

who are unregistered but that could make healthy, fine pets. Yes, it's confusing, but ask anyway, to get the employees talking about the dog, the breeder, and the origin. The more questions you ask about the store's source for puppies, the more you might be able to find out about the breeder's priorities and history.

WESTIE COMES HOME

After considering how adding a pup or adult dog will affect your family, you come to an enthusiastic consensus about purchasing or rescuing your Westie. Now it's time to bring your little white bundle of joy home. If possible, schedule your newcomer's arrival on a weekend or during vacation in order to spend time with the new puppy.

Puppy Proof Like it's Going Out of Style

Your house is a cornucopia of both dangerous and valuable items. Within your adorable, innocent Westie rests the potential to destroy anything "by any means necessary." I have verifiable reports of Westies having swallowed 9-volt batteries, disposable razors, air conditioner plugs, and bubbler-head sprinklers—sometimes to the tune of hundred of dollars in veterinary bills. And as for the years whittled off owners' lives—priceless!

Electrical cords, poisonous plants, antifreeze, cosmetics, and cleaning supplies, which can be extremely hazardous, are attractive to dogs—especially puppies. Keep holiday decorations out of your Westie's reach. Never burn candles where he can get to them. Keep cellar doors and upper-story windows closed. Trash should be inaccessible to your dog. Be extremely cautious if you use insecticides, pesticides, or chemical fertilizers. (Better yet, avoid them altogether.) Keep printed literature out of reach. Westies are intelligent, but their idea of "devouring books" is more literal than ours.

Indefinite Listing Privilege Program (ILP)

A purebred dog may be ineligible for conventional AKC registration for many reasons. Her litter may be unregistered, she may have unregistered parents, or her papers may be lost. Surrendered or abandoned dogs adopted by new owners from animal shelters or rescue groups may come without papers. The ILP program allows dog and owner the opportunity to participate in all approved AKC performance and companion activities—except for conformation. You can download an ILP application from www.akc.org or contact the AKC and request a form.

A securely fenced yard is a necessity with a Westie.

Fencing

One of the first things a good Westie breeder will ask you is, "Do you have a securely fenced yard?" Stockade is more like it. Westies are terriers—perfectly capable of digging their own "underground railroads" to freedom. A chain-link fence of at least 4 or 5 feet (1.2 m) (yes, some Westies can climb) reinforced at the bottom and secured with a padlock works well.

Invisible fences fit your dog with a special collar that delivers a shock when he attempts to cross the boundary of your yard. These fences are a poor choice for a small dog like the Westie. First of all, these fences don't keep other dogs or people from crossing the boundary into your yard. Second, terriers are particularly prey-driven, and the choice between a temporary shock and bagging a squirrel may be a no-brainer to a Westie. Once out, he's not likely to cross back through that barrier again. Third, the collars can malfunction and shock your dog during an outage.

Timing

As a rule, "Christmas puppies" are a bad idea. With all the holiday activity and the visitors, one would be hard-pressed to find a more stressful time for new dogs and new owners. The exception is a quiet household that doesn't make much

Naming Your Westie

Here are a few tips for picking the perfect moniker for your new Westie. If you have multiple pets, make sure that their names sound distinct enough as to not cause confusion. If your first one is named "Sharon," don't name your next one "Darrin." Some owners recommend that you select a name that ends with either an a (as in the name "Cara") or an o (as in the name "Elmo") The long e sound also works well. Names ending with long vowel sounds are easier for your dog to hear, since they carry well over longer distances. Some people like to name a Westie to match his heritage. Books on naming a baby or websites that list Scottish names abound.

Some people name their dogs according to their physical traits or personality. There aren't many Westies named "Spot" or "Ebony." But some names arise spontaneously. When an adorable Westie puppy urinated on the lap of Oregon Westie breeder Mary Lou Ludlow, little "Peony" unwittingly chose her own name.

Names that mean "fair" or "white" are plentiful for these beautiful white terriers: Alban, Blanche, Bianca, Guinevere, Jennifer, Berrin, Gandolf, Bevin, Banya, Muriel, Leigan, Kennan, Keevin, and Finola are all possibilities. Scottish names with associations to the words white or clouds or brightness include Alpin, Ceana, Fiona, Sorcha, Fingal, Findlay, Lilias, and Kenna.

It's important to only invoke your Westie's name in association with something positive. You don't want to yell, "Here, Cloudy! Come here and let's express your anal glands!" or your Westie will simply stop coming to you.

of the holidays. Spring and summer can be optimal for housetraining, but puppies are born in their own time—and if you're committed, you can make any time work.

Leaving his mother, home, and littermates is one of the great stresses in a puppy's young life. The stimulus flooding of a new home, new people, and even new pets can be intense. But given your patience and compassion, your puppy will quickly bond with his new family. Remember also that puppies need lots of sleep, so resist the temptation to overload your Westie with too much excitement; you'll both be happier. Keeping him on his former routine can soften the transition. Continue to feed him at the same time and place every day, and all will be well. Set up your Westie's crate in a special place in the house—this will be his refuge. Never use this spot to punish the dog.

The First Night

Your Westie puppy's first night may be traumatic for him. It is strange for him to be away from his family and littermates, so why not let him spend the night with you (in his crate) in your bedroom? By doing this, you will stay attuned to any stirring that could indicate he needs to relieve himself. As you head out in your nightshirt and nightcap into the starry, starry night, know that this can help expedite the housebreaking process.

He may cry a lot. Just talk to him in a soothing voice as he drifts off again. At the beginning, you may miss a few z's before he sleeps through the night, but there is light at the end of the tunnel. Try putting a few of your T-shirts in his crate. This will comfort, pacify, and make his initial night's sleep less stressful.

Introducing Your Westie to Other Pets

If you already have another dog, Deb Duncan—trainer, behaviorist, and Westie owner—recommends setting up the new dog's "personal effects" about a week before introducing the little interloper to your first dog. This helps your first dog acclimate to the physical changes in his environment. "Prior to bringing home the new pup or dog, try, if possible, to bring home a towel or a T-shirt with the 'new' dog's scent on it. Place it where your current dog can investigate it. Arrange to expose your new dog to an item with your present dog's smell," suggests Duncan.

Allow the two future roomies to meet on neutral territory. Don't be shocked if your current dog regresses in his housetraining or manners. Duncan stresses that ignoring this behavior is the best way to reduce the anxiety that causes it. Create situations where you can reward or pay attention to both dogs simultaneously. This helps diminish any latent "sibling rivalry" and reinforces the idea that good things happen when the two are together. Treat and praise in tandem.

If you have a cat, you'll want to prevent cat-o-mania. Separate the new pup from your cat until the pup is tired. Make the initial, supervised introduction or get-acquainted visit when the pup's energy is depleted. If your cat is extremely testy, consult with your veterinarian about mild sedation for the feline. Observation: It is definitely easier when the cat is there first.

SUPPLIES!

Here are a few essentials you'll need for your new addition.

Food and Water

Your Westie requires a high-quality, nutritionally balanced diet, and fresh, clean water at all times. Common wisdom suggests that you obtain—from the breeder, shelter, or rescue

No Tie-Outs!

Chaining your Westie outside to a stake in the ground (called a tie-out) not only deprives him of love, training, and attention, but it is cruel and can be dangerous. Westies are social creatures—they want to be with you, not alone in a yard.

worker—a transitional supply of the food the dog has been eating and continue feeding the same food. Abruptly changing your Westie's food can result in diarrhea and general gastric upset. If you opt to change foods, do it on a half-and-half basis for the first week—and keep him on a high quality food. (High quality does not mean "performance" food, unless you're planning to add your Westie to an Iditarod team.) A cheap dog food is lower in essential nutrients than the pricier brands, so you may end up at the vet's spending any money you save. Feed only the best quality food with whole ingredients and natural preservatives.

What to serve your Westie's food in? Inexpensive, durable, and easy to clean stainless steel food and water dishes work best. Avoid plastic bowls; they're incubators for bacteria. Ceramic bowls, though breakable, work well too.

Collar and Leash

An adjustable, lightweight collar made of either leather or nylon, with a secure clasp or a buckle is the best choice. A "choke" or a "slip" collar is inappropriate and dangerous for everyday wear. These types of collars tighten around your dog's neck, and if caught on something can seriously injure or strangle the dog. Collars of this type are used in some training methods, and should only be used by professionals.

The best leashes are 4 to 6 feet/1.2 m long and made of leather or nylon. Quality leather leashes are comfortable, last a long time, and break in like a good pair of loafers. Cheap ones can chafe your hands. Do not allow your Westie to mouth or chew on the leash or he'll quickly acquire a taste for it. Taste deterrents such as Bitter Apple may discourage such experimentation.

Bed

A bed can be made of any soft, washable material. Many dogs find the faux sheepskin type very comfortable. If you'd like something more basic, plain towels or T-shirts that carry your scent work fine. Avoid wicker—a Westie puppy can easily transform it into a dangerous chew-fest.

Crate

An important housetraining tool and general all-purpose den for your Westie, a crate is arguably the mother of all dog

---

Westie Gift Certificate

If you must give a puppy as a Christmas gift, and the breeder insists (rightly) on delaying his homecoming, try this: Make a "Westie gift certificate." Incorporate a picture of the puppy you'll be adopting into a card. Buy a crate and fill it with a baby (temporary) collar, a few squeaky toys, stainless steel food and water bowls, and perhaps a tiny chew like a Nylabone. Be creative, and don't forget to include a book on West Highland White Terriers—like this one!

A baby gate can provide necessary safety for your Westie.

supplies: a refuge, a safe travel container, a convalescent haven, a time-out place—and at ten o'clock you will know where your Westie is! Whether to select a plastic, wire mesh, or solid oak crate is up to you.

Exercise Pen (Ex-pen)

An ex-pen is a portable wire playpen for your dog. Perfect for traveling or for confining him to a small area of the house, an ex-pen allows you to keep tabs on each other.

Dog Door

A dog door that opens into a securely fenced yard makes life (and often housetraining) a breeze. Your Westie won't need your permission to go outside. Easy to install, the most common type has a clear plastic panel that opens easily and closes with magnets. Like most gadgets, they come in different grades and qualities.

Toys

Safe toys have parts that won't detach. Rubber toys provide the best jaw and mouth exercise—they're ideal for chewers and dogs that spend a lot of time alone. Hard, hollow, rubber beehive-shaped toys are popular with most

dogs. Stuff the hollow middle with treats such as peanut butter, canned cheese, or biscuits. Vinyl squeaky toys also work well for the more tentative chewers. Plush toys pick up different smells, so dogs are fond of these, but some dogs seem determined to disembowel stuffed toys. Watch out for squeakers, which can be dangerous. Flavored floss toys can keep teeth and gums in shape. Nylon bones like Nylabones are sturdy and beneficial and come infused with appealing flavors. Discard any toy that gets reduced to a size your Westie can swallow.

Don't overdo it. Too many toys can lead to a jaded, bored Westie, but a few well-chosen ones can keep him from destroying your pricey footwear or handbags. It's amazing how quickly Jimmy Choos can be transformed, much to your horror, into "Jimmy Chews," or your beloved black Prada bag to "nada."

Baby Gates

When you don't want your Westie playing unsupervised in your house, a baby gate can provide the necessary barrier. It may also prevent your puppy from stumbling down (or ascending) steep stairs.

Cleaning Supplies

Rags, paper towels, and enzymatic cleaners made for cleaning up pet "mistakes" are good to have on hand. White vinegar works well for cleaning out plastic crates.

IDENTIFYING YOUR DOG

Provide your Westie with a flat collar and tag that carries your name, address, and phone number. Some collars allow you to write information with a laundry marker, so that even if the tags fall off, he can still be identified.

Microchipping

Microchips provide positive and reliable identification for your pet. A chip about the size of a grain of rice is painlessly inserted into your pet. Modern shelters, veterinarians, and humane societies can scan animals for this ID device. Find out which brand of chip is most used in your area and go with that one. Usually, there is a central database that houses the chip's ID number, so you can notify the company if you or your Westie relocates. However, the microchip should not replace a traditional ID tag.

Tattooing

Tattoos also provide positive identification when done correctly. The best place to apply a tattoo is on the inner thigh, where it will be visible.

What to Do If Your Westie Is Lost

Hopefully, you will never have to go through the trauma of a lost dog. But in case it does happen, do should do the following:

- Keep on file current photographs of your Westie for identification purposes. Including yourself in some of the photos helps establish your ownership.
- Always have a current rabies tag and identification tag attached to your pet's collar. You can be found by the number on the tags. Animals without identification are often euthanized after a relatively short time. Identification buys time.
- Small dogs can get into some weird and tiny places, so search your property thoroughly. Look everywhere—inside appliances, inside pipes, and under anything! A frightened or injured dog will hide in dark spaces, so bring a flashlight. Check under houses, in storage sheds, garages, dumpsters, trash cans, and under cars.
- Gather your whole family to call your Westie's name. Use a dog whistle to get your pet's attention. The high-pitched sound from these whistles can carry up to a mile or more. Stop, be quiet, and listen for your pet to "reply."
- Troll the neighborhood: Talk to the residents of each house in the area where your pet was lost. Leave with them a written description of your pet and your phone number. Because of scam artists, never leave your full name or address.
- Call and visit all of the local shelters and animal control agencies. Many have computerized lost and found information, but it's up to you to go to the shelter to check out any leads in person. Walk through the kennels; don't assume that telephoning is sufficient.
- Check listings of animals left at local veterinarians' offices; leave behind a flyer and a picture.

Did You Know?

Self-stick door/window signs for emergency workers, and emergency-contact stickers provide vital information regarding your dog such as your name, your dog's vet, and your neighbors' contact information. You can acquire these through the US Humane Society.

- File a lost report with the local animal control agency. Attach a current picture of your Westie to the file card, and be sure to call to have the card removed when you locate your dog.
- Post flyers within a mile radius of the place the dog was lost. Posting flyers results in more found pets than any other method. Be sure to include a color photo of your Westie. List the date and place you last saw him, his breed, sex, age, and weight, along with your telephone number. But do withhold several distinguishing characteristics of your dog. If the person who claims to have found your pet cannot describe these features to you, they do not have your pet.
- Check the "found" ads in newspapers and place a "lost" ad.
- Ask elementary schools in your area to post flyers. Kids are everywhere and may see your dog.
- Talk to everybody you run across and give them your Westie's description and your phone number. Neighborhood kids are a great resource.
- Talk to local businesses, your letter carrier, sanitation workers, and your neighbors.
- Call radio stations that offer lost-pet notices as a public service.
- Notify the local Westie Club.
- In all instances, offer a reward, but avoid revealing the amount.
- Don't ever give up. Lost dogs have been known to return home after months!

TRAVELING WITH YOUR WESTIE

The Westie's size makes him very easy to take along with you wherever you go.

By Car

Leaving your Westie loose in the car is dangerous. The safest way to travel in a car with your precious cargo is to place him in his crate with a blanket, pad, or towel in the backseat. To prevent the crate from shifting, use either the seatbelt or bungee cords.

There are also special harness-style seatbelts that you can use in combination with the car seatbelts. This gives your dog

Car Safety

Never allow your Westie to dangle his head out the window. Perils include close-moving vehicles that can graze your dog, airborne particles that can harm eyes, and automatic windows carelessly kept unlocked (so that the dog can inadvertently operate them).

Make sure your Westie's ID tags are up to date before you travel.

a safe alternative to roaming, posing on the dashboard as an ornament, sitting on your lap in order to influence your driving, working the automatic windows (which can be dangerous and distracting), or wending his way on the floor toward the gas pedal under your feet—the perfect den in his mind. However, Westies are problem solvers, and some escape artists have found ways to extricate themselves from seat belts. (Most, however, are incapable of unlatching their crates.) When buying the harness, get your dog's measurements and weight. If you take the dog with you, you can try the harness out on him in the store. A Westie will usually wear a small or medium, depending on the brand. Practice putting your dog in his harness. Once you've purchased it, allow him to wear it around the house until he no longer notices it.

Getting Your Westie Adjusted to Car Travel

Some techniques might help your Westie adjust to car travel. The younger he starts, the better. Either harness or crate your puppy in the backseat, and take a short ride. When he's quiet, reinforce that behavior with a treat. Extend the duration of your trips, making sure they're frequently associated with positive places—the pet-supply store, the park, a play date with another dog—so as to overshadow the trips to those places not on his wish list. If you're using a harness and he tangles it, simply readjust it—and continue on. Be as tenacious as he is, and all will work out. Use the same methods with an adult dog as you would with a puppy. For particularly tough cases, just proceed more gradually and with more patience.

Car Sickness

Most Westies love car rides, but you may have one prone to car sickness. This can arise either from insecurity or from some physical tendency. Short car rides can help puppies adjust to this aspect of car travel. Take your puppy on an empty stomach, and provide lots of fresh air by opening a window. Start short and work toward longer trips. Many pups will fall asleep in their crates. Also, natural and homeopathic remedies for car sickness are available online or at health food stores; these are effective for some dogs. You may obtain prescription pills or give a car sickness medicine as per vet instructions, but if the sickness is so severe that your Westie needs sedation, you're better off leaving him home.

By Air

Because of your Westie's size, you have the option of having him travel with you in an airplane's cabin. When you make arrangements for your flight, inform the agent that you are traveling with your dog. Check back to ensure that both reservations are confirmed; airlines usually only allow one or two pets in the cabin. Your carry-on dog-carrier bag must be airline approved. Weight requirements vary with each airline, but the dog must always fit comfortably into his carrier. He needs enough room to stand up and turn around, and the bag must fit under the seat. Westies generally travel quite well; many are lulled to sleep by the whirring of the plane's engine.

Before your flight, your Westie will require some prior exposure to the carrier bag. Start by opening the bag and placing some treats in it so that he'll enter it of his own volition. Leave it out, and let him get accustomed to the pleasant associations. Eventually, let him go inside with the treat, and zip up the bag. If he's sedate enough, start carrying it around the room while praising him constantly. Then carry the bag to the car and take him for a short ride. Continue the praise and up the ante—taking him into a store or a building in the bag. As he adjusts, add more distractions and situations—such as elevators and noisy places.

Consider tranquilizers only as a last resort for a super-anxious dog, since they can interfere with breathing. If tranquilizing is inevitable, confer with your vet about trying the medication once before the flight to ensure your Westie doesn't react adversely. You don't want a surprise like that when you're in the air where your dog cannot get medical attention.

Also, consider the following tips for before and during the cabin flight:

- Bathe and groom him to reduce dander, smells, and allergens.
- Potty and exercise him before you get to the airport, and arrive there no earlier than necessary.
- Trim his nails so that they do not catch on the mesh of the carrier or—if he's in cargo—on any wire of the kennel.
- Withhold food and water for a few hours before boarding.
- At the airport, keep your dog in his bag—except in designated areas.
- Acquire a health certificate from your vet; at check-in time, the airline agent will request it. This is proof that your pet is fit to travel and current with his rabies vaccination.
- Once you've boarded, place the carrier under the seat. Don't unzip the bag—Westies are quick, and your little jack-in-the-box will pop out in less than a New York minute. If you need to slip him a morsel of food or water while in flight, wait until after the onboard food service has ended.
- If your layover requires leaving the plane, ask a flight attendant or other airline employee if there is an area where your Westie may relieve himself.

Airline flight regulations in regard to pets change almost constantly. For more specific information about particular airlines, go to www.akc.org/news/airline_chart_0504.pdf.

Staying at a Hotel or Motel

Many hotels and motels offer accommodations to people traveling with small pets. Online, you can check

Travel Tips

- On long trips, provide your Westie with a stretch and a potty break (on a leash) at least every four hours.
- Some owners have found that feeding their carsick puppy a gingersnap or two can settle his stomach. (And you, too, can enjoy a snack.)

A kennel or pet sitter may be good options when you can't take your Westie with you.

www.takeyourpet.com. Books are available with comparable information, but the websites tend to be most up-to-date.

In the hotel room, be courteous and practice etiquette. When you go out and leave your dog in the room, turn on the TV. (Animal Planet is a good choice.) Set up his food and water in the bathroom—or some other noncarpeted area. Ask the hotel if they use any antipest products, and if they do, find them and remove them. Always clean up after your dog—inside and outside. If you've got a male Westie who enjoys leaving "liquid mail," consider buying and bringing a bellyband or cummerbund. There are many venues, including dog shows, that sell these ingenious items.

IF YOU CAN'T TAKE YOUR WESTIE WITH YOU

If you're going to explore the Galapagos Islands, attend the Academy Awards, or bicycle across the United States, your Westie may be unable to accompany you, so you'll have to figure out how to provide for his care. Some breeders willingly board any dog they've bred, or a friend or relative might offer to take care of your Westie during your absence. But not everyone is that fortunate.

Boarding Kennels

A dog with medical issues needing attention and regular medication may do best in a vet clinic that boards dogs. For a normal, healthy Westie, consider a boarding kennel. But before committing, request a tour. And during holidays and summers, many kennels are booked up for months in advance, so plan ahead.

Ask your vet or other dog owners for boarding recommendations. Any facility you consider for your Westie should meet the following criteria:

- It should be clean.
- It should have both indoor and outdoor runs.
- It should allow dogs opportunities for exercise and play.
- It should offer grooming and bathing facilities.
- It should require proof of health and vaccination.
- It should have easy and dependable access to veterinary services.

A good kennel will allow you to bring your Westie's food, toys, and bedding, if you choose. They'll provide climate control as needed. When in doubt, check to see if the facility is accredited with the American Boarding Kennel Association.

Pet Sitter

Some pet sitting services will house-sit as well as pet-sit; others will make arrangements to come in and walk, feed, and play with your dog. If you are considering this option, meet the caretaker first and observe how he or she interacts with your Westie. Ask for references and inquire about experience. Ask how the caretaker might handle certain emergencies and how many clients he or she cares for at once. Set up a specific schedule together for caring for your dog. Provide instructions on how to get in touch with you and your vet and any other pertinent information.

Doggy Daycare

"Doggy daycare" is a place where, while *you* work or play, your Westie can socialize with dogs of compatible temperament, burn off excess canine energy in monitored playgroups, and interact with people outside his own family. At best, it can help build your Westie's confidence and reinforce training and good manners.

If you choose this option, make sure the provider realizes that the rough-and-tumble, growly playing typical of Westies and other terriers is perfectly appropriate and not a sign of abnormal aggression.

FEEDING

YOUR WEST HIGHLAND
WHITE TERRIER

Y ou may have noticed that your Westie likes to eat pretty much anything. Although he's technically classified as a carnivore, or meat eater, he'll even eat (what you'll see as) garbage if you allow him. So it's up to you to feed him a good, nutritious diet, and provide him with fresh, clean water at all times.

When it comes to food, the choice is practically unlimited: dry food, canned food, semimoist, home-cooked human food, species-appropriate raw food (ARF), or any mixture thereof. Factors that influence your choice are convenience, expense, nutritional value, taste, availability, allergies, and whether you like the human resources and animal practices of the company that manufactures a food. What's appropriate for one dog and owner may not be appropriate for another.

Avoid feeding your Westie anything he hates. How would you like to be offered deep-fried lard burgers for every meal? Sure, he'll eat almost anything (even the lard burgers) rather than starve. But mealtimes should be fun and festive for everyone, so why not go the extra mile and find something nutritious that your dog really enjoys? If he likes something for a while and then tires of it, just change it. (Gradually, of course.)

COMMERCIAL DOG FOODS

Mere dollars a bag separate the best and worst commercial foods, but the disparity in quality is priceless. Feeding a top-of-the-line food can make all the difference in the world when it comes to your Westie's well-being.

Dogs have been eating ready-to-eat foods only since World War II, when the army needed a convenient, easy-to-store food for its dogs of war, so it developed K-9 rations to accompany its K rations. Today, a vast majority of American dog owners feed their dog primarily or solely a commercial diet—usually dry kibble. (There has, however, been a growing trend toward alternative diets.) Many of these cheaper products contain barely enough nutrients to be considered "nutritionally complete," so many of them are not particularly ideal nourishment for your dog. Their greatest advantage is their convenience.

Digestive problems are typical of a dog fed a poor-quality kibble, canned, or soft, moist processed dog food. Symptoms of digestive upset include flatulence, copious and odiferous stools, diarrhea, several bowel movements per day, halitosis, and frequent vomiting.

Some newer premium products come close to top nutrition, but you probably won't find them in grocery stores. More and more pet stores are offering them, or you can get them online. Some companies will deliver food right to your door. Also, there's been some growth in the holistic pet movement, and there are stores that specialize in high-quality, organic, and all-natural pet food.

Fortunately, the highly competitive dog food market is driving up the overall quality of commercial foods. More decent choices exist than ever before, but it's up to consumers to educate themselves about what they're buying. So how do you know what food is best for your Westie? Start with the label.

Reading the Label

Understanding any food label can be confusing. Still, the careful consumer can decipher at least some of it. Federal regulations require shockingly little of pet food manufacturers. Companies are only obligated to accurately identify the product, provide the net quantity, give an address, and correctly list the ingredients. But they're exempt from quality control laws.

At the very least, look for the Association of American Feed Control Officials (AAFCO) label. This organization provides some very basic standards that pet foods must meet in order to carry its endorsement. AAFCO-labeled foods provide a guaranteed analysis of the food, calorie statement, and a "nutritional adequacy statement." This in no way ensures quality: It just means that the food is properly labeled.

Start with the nutritional adequacy statement. This tells you for which life stage (growth, pregnancy, lactation, and/or adult) the food is intended. It also tells you how the pet food manufacturer has verified the food's adequacy. For instance, the label might say that the food was tested either by feeding trials or by chemical analysis. AAFCO sets the guidelines for feeding trials. When a food has been tested through feeding trials, it at least proves that some dogs have eaten it for six months without dying or getting sick. (Not all that reassuring.) But it beats chemical analysis' attempt to show that the food contains the same basic chemical components as foods that have actually been tested. This

practice benefits the company's bottom line more than it does your dog. Neither feeding trials nor chemical analyses reveal much about the actual quality of the food.

Remember to provide your Westie with plenty of fresh water.

Dry Food (Kibble)

Kibble can be a convenient, nutritionally adequate dog food. Dry food can help reduce tartar buildup on teeth, although it's no substitute for proper dental hygiene. However, it doesn't clean the canine teeth, since dogs chew it with their molars (that is, if they don't simply bolt it down). Compared to other feeding options, basic kibble is the least expensive, primarily due to its high grain content. Dry food tends to be low in fat, an advantage if your dog is overweight or a couch potato. Fancy colors and shapes may appeal to humans, but your Westie couldn't care less. Have you ever heard any dog rejoice, "Would you check this out? A purple rainbow!"

Many, but not all, dry food companies use BHA or BHT as preservatives. Until recently, ethoxyquin (originally a rubber hardener developed in the 1950s) was commonly used in both human and dog foods, but due to increasing consumer pressure, in 1998 the FDA proclaimed ethoxyquin unsafe for human food. It cannot legally be used to preserve human food, since some fairly compelling evidence links it to cancer, liver disease, and immune disorders. However, it is still being used in a few pet products. Fortunately, an increasing number of companies are switching to vitamin E as a natural and effective preservative. Play it safe by opting for those foods.

Other things to consider if feeding a conventional kibble-based diet: Westies, unlike other larger working breeds, thrive on a diet that is lower in protein. Kibble varies in its percentage of protein and fat and fat-to-protein ratios, so check the label. If you feed a product with 21 percent protein, the fat content should be at least a 10.5 percent or greater. The higher fat content helps lubricate a drier coat, a common problem in Westies.

Canned Food

Although canned dog food smells, well, like dog food to us, given a choice, most dogs would choose it over dry. However, canned food is considerably pricier than kibble. To find the best canned food for your dog, look for one containing whole meat, fish, or poultry as the first ingredient. Most inferior canned foods list water as the first ingredient. (And with non-AAFCO foods, you never know.) You rarely find premium canned foods at your supermarket. You can find better-quality food via the manufacturer, pet stores, or even dog shows.

Canned food usually contains about 75 percent water. The maximum amount of water allowed in AAFCO-labeled canned food is 78 percent. (However, if the food is labeled as "gravy," "sauce," or "stew," the water content may exceed that.) Some canned dog food contains grain products; some contains only meat. Whether or not grain products benefit dogs is controversial. The best canned foods use whole veggies instead of "grain fractions" such as rice bran, rice flour, or brewer's rice. Since dogs, though primarily carnivorous, are on the cusp of omnivorous, fresh vegetables add necessary nutrients to their regime.

High in fat, canned food is often best used by mixing it with dry food, especially if your dog needs a taste enhancer. Due to the increased water content of the food, dogs with urinary tract infections frequently do better on canned dog foods than on kibble.

Semimoist Food

Semimoist food contains about 25 percent water and just as much sugar, in its many guises: corn syrup, beet pulp, sucrose, and/or caramel. Sugar promotes obesity and tooth decay. The shelf life of these products is lower than either canned or dry food. Semimost food is not usually recommended for Westies.

Picking the Best Commercial Food

Almost any kind of meat can end up in dog food. In many places, pet food manufacturers are free to use road kill, diseased cattle, or any other source of protein that tickles their fancy. Fortunately, some companies use only human-grade meat. Companies were not formerly permitted to state this valuable fact on their labels. However, this regulation has now been changed, so you can easily choose human-grade meats for your dog.

For the best nutritional options, stick to the following simple guidelines:

- Avoid dog foods containing "by-products." Meat by-products are the part of the animal not deemed fit for human consumption.
- Avoid food overloaded with grain or cereal by-products. These ingredients are the part of the plant left over after the milling process. Technically called "fragments," they appear on labels in many aliases. Carbohydrates in food should be whole grains.
- Stay away from soy, which many dogs are allergic to.
- If you feed kibble, choose a type preserved naturally with vitamin E (tocopherols) or vitamin C (ascorbic acid). Healthful dog food should not contain sweeteners, artificial flavors, colors, or preservatives.
- Select food with the specific name of a meat ("beef," "chicken," "turkey") as the first ingredient. Avoid foods whose label lists a generic "meat" or "poultry." Also be aware that just because a product has "beef" listed as the first ingredient doesn't mean the product is mostly beef. Some companies engage in a deceptive practice called "splitting." If they can possibly do so, they will divide the cereal products up into separate categories, like "rice" and then "brown rice." Added together, there will be more grain fragment than beef. But because the companies are allowed

Feeding Tips

- Some people feed their dogs a basic kibble diet and enhance it by adding different foods every day: green beans, carrots, gravy, or canned meat for extra nutrition and variety.
- Often, dog food bags carry the recommendation that you feed your Westie enough food to sustain Bigfoot. Talk to your vet about how much food your Westie really needs for each stage of life.
- Serve food at room temperature if possible. Very cold food eaten rapidly can make a dog vomit. Some dogs prefer food if it's slightly warmed.

If you are feeding your dog a commercial diet, make sure it is high quality.

to list them as separate ingredients, beef is listed first.

Be sure that any foods you feed your dog do not have any of the following on the label:

- Meat by-products.
- Chicken by-products.
- Fats or proteins named generically such as "animal fat" or "poultry fat." Instead look for "beef fat" or "chicken fat" or "lamb meal."
- Food fragments such as brewer's rice, corn gluten, etc.
- Artificial colors.
- Sweeteners including corn syrup, sucrose, and ammoniated glycyrrhizin, added to attract dogs to otherwise unappealing food.
- Propylene glycol. This toxin is added to some "chewy" foods to keep them moist.
- Artificial preservatives such as BHA, BHT, and ethoxyquin.

Any one of the above can cause dogs to vomit, or worse, to develop health problems over time.

NONCOMMERCIAL DIETS

Appropriate Raw Food (ARF)

Raw, natural diets have steadily gained popularity (and spurred much controversy) over the last several years. Some vets are adamantly opposed; others support them or maintain a wait-and-see attitude. Many holistic practitioners wholeheartedly endorse the diets.

Raw feeding/natural rearing advocate Christine Swingle, a Westie breeder and exhibitor for over forty years, points out that dogs have short digestive systems, designed to digest food quickly. This means they are well suited to digesting raw meat and bones and will stay healthy on a species-appropriate raw-food diet (ARF).

Swingle and others correlate the general decline in canine health to improper diets. For example, cancer is now the leading medical cause of death in all dogs, but forty years ago, cancer was uncommon. Additionally, autoimmune disease is on the rise, and more than 85 percent of all dogs will, by age three, manifest some level of periodontal disease. A healthy immune system and digestive system start with the foods we feed. They're the foundation for wellness.

Much, though not all, processed commercial dog food is a concoction of grains, cereals, chemicals, and dyes. A great way to recycle society's waste and very convenient for the increasingly busy and overworked consumer, these products mainly benefit the burgeoning pet food industry, which profits handsomely. Raw food, full of live enzymes, is digested quickly, and the nutrients are utilized with greater efficiency.

Storing Food

Improperly stored food can become breeding grounds for molds and toxins, some deadly. Buy only the freshest foods available. If you use a commercial food, check the manufacturing date. With a small breed like a Westie, you're best off buying in small bags. Buying in bulk may save you some money, but in the long run the money you save on food may end up going to your vet. Smaller bags get used more quickly, which means the food stays fresher.

Store the food in a dry, cool place away from sunlight. Keep the food in the house or in another place with a stable temperature. Temperature fluctuations can produce moisture in the food storage container and encourage the development of mold or toxins. Store the food in its original packaging or in a special airtight container. Don't use a plastic garbage can—even clean plastics can produce dangerous vapors.

If the food smells bad, or if your dog suddenly refuses to eat it—even though he appears hungry enough to chew his own feet off, discard the food, or return it for a refund.

Swingle stresses that learning to feed raw food correctly is absolutely crucial to anyone planning to attempt such a diet. Feeding a raw-food diet, although easy to master, requires extra thought, understanding, research, and knowledge. Without this understanding, converting to an ARF diet can be tricky and even dangerous, especially if the appropriate foods are not fed over a week's time. Before starting your Westie on ARF, make sure you read up on the subject. The resources section at the end of this book contains some titles for suggested reading. Swingle also recommends, if possible, joining an online support group and continuing to learn as much as possible.

If you feed your dog raw meat, obtain the freshest cuts available. For example, chicken necks and wings have a perfect calcium/phosphorus ratio. But common bacterial components of raw meat may include campylobacterosis, E. coli, listeriosis, salmonellosis, trichinosis, and tapeworm. Protozoan infections are also possible. Still, it's rare for a dog to contract these diseases, since a healthy dog's system is essentially equipped to handle them.

The most dangerous consequence of bone consumption is a perforated intestine, which allows toxins to escape into the dog's system. Even some raw bones can splinter when dogs chew them and can puncture the esophagus or stomach. One way to reduce this risk is to grind the bones thoroughly or feed a commercially prepared raw diet.

What you include in a raw diet over a week's time is important. With the right guidance and information, it is not that difficult. It is important to feed a properly rounded raw diet. Excessive dairy, too many vegetables (a few will suffice), or extra grains and cereals (there is some debate here) are not recommended. Misuse of supplements can also thwart correct nutritional balance.

A raw diet isn't a cure-all. A switch to raw repast is no guarantee that all health issues will disappear. Diet merely supports and promotes good health. Although digestive and some other problems often clear up with ARF, diet alone cannot restore health.

Yet there are many positive results of feeding ARF, as follows:
- reduction or absence of tartar on teeth and healthy gums
- small, odorless stools

- absence of flatulence
- anal glands that generally "self-express"
- easier weight control and better muscular condition
- elimination of bad breath

Switching from processed dog food to raw food should be gradual, as should any diet change. Also, some dogs simply cannot regain sufficient digestive health to tolerate ARF. In those cases, a high-quality kibble, supplemented by digestive enzymes and raw grated veggies, is a good choice.

A home-cooked diet can be tailored to your dog's specific needs.

Home-Cooked Meals

Many people opt to prepare their dog's diet at home. You can tailor the diet to his particular needs, and you'll be using quality ingredients that exclude artificial preservatives and by-products. Home-cooked diets are more expensive than commercial ones, but you can offset the cost by including healthy leftovers from your own meals with your Westie's.

Preparing a diet at home does require vigilance and training. The main perils of such diets are calcium/phosphorus imbalance and inadequate levels of calcium, copper, iodine, and certain vitamins—especially the fat-soluble ones and some of the B vitamins. People who feed their dogs a diet of fresh meat without the bone and vegetables must supplement the food with a calcium source like bone meal. The correct amount is difficult to gauge, and some bone meal supplements contain dangerously high levels of lead. In this regard, you are probably safer using a commercially prepared food or feeding raw meaty bones. Many excellent books contain nourishing homemade diets that you can adapt to your own purposes.

People Food

It's not a crime to feed your dog most foods that are healthy for human beings. "Don't feed your dog table scraps" was part of a slick propaganda campaign perpetuated by dog food manufacturers. Dogs thrive on fresh vegetables, chicken, beef, and fish. Many dogs also like fruits, including apple slices, melons, bananas, and berries. (Mine adore the seedless mandarins they receive in their Christmas stockings every year.) Low-fat plain yogurt and small amounts of cottage cheese are also delightful treats and add a bit of calcium. However, most dogs don't have the necessary enzymes to process large quantities of dairy.

Neither you nor your Westie needs cookies, potato chips, donuts, or pork rinds. Many of these cause gastrointestinal upset, not to mention obesity. Hopefully your dog is unaccustomed to high-fat foods; several organs in a dog's body can be stressed from eating these, and pancreatitis, which is potentially fatal, can also result.

Very young puppies need to eat several times a day.

AGE-APPROPRIATE FEEDING

Puppies

Very young puppies (two to four months) need to eat three or four times a day—their rapid development of mind and body require extra fortification. Usually a high-quality growth formula kibble softened with some warm water is best. You can add some yogurt, canola or corn oil, or cottage cheese for palatability. Follow the instructions of your breeder and/or vet.

Let your baby Westie eat as little or as much of his portion as he chooses. Pick up unfinished food after about ten minutes. Coaxing, cajoling, or adding *pâté de fois gras* will only make him finicky, and he'll be wondering why any dog would eat dog food unless stranded on a desert island.

Around six months, start feeding two meals—breakfast and dinner. At a year, you may want to reduce it to once a day, although some owners choose to stick with two meals.

Feed your baby Westie in a quiet place away from brouhaha and other pets. You can also feed him in his crate, which will reinforce the crate as a safe place. In any case, your puppy should get accustomed to your close presence while he eats. He should learn that you control his food. If he growls, remove his food until he stops the inappropriate behavior. This is the best way to discourage food-guarding. However, tempting fate by allowing children or others to hassle the dog while he's eating is unfair.

Adults

The right time to make the switch from puppy chow to adult formula can easily vary from Westie to Westie. Generally, by the time he is nine months to a year old, it's time for the transition. However, if your Westie is looking rotund at five or six months, he may be ready for adult food—that is, if you are not overfeeding him. (Package recommendations tend to be "generous"—both to your puppy's girth and to the manufacturer.) Your Westie's feeding requirements will vary with his individual metabolism and level of activity. Ask your vet if you have any questions about how much to feed your Westie.

Free Feeding Versus Scheduled Feeding

You have the choice of feeding your adult Westie on a

Food Desire as a Training Opportunity

Food can be a tool—a reward for good behavior—that helps your Westie associate pleasing you with pleasing himself. But there is a subtle difference between using food as a bribe and as a reward. A Westie who is not food-motivated is a rare find, but if yours is more motivated by a favorite toy or a tennis ball, use whatever works.

schedule, or "free feeding," which means leaving food out all day. In most cases, dogs should be fed on a schedule—once or twice a day, if they are being fed a high-quality commercial adult food. Although feeding on a schedule is slightly more time-consuming than free feeding, it gives you much more control over what your Westie is eating.

Free feeding is strongly linked to obesity. It's hard to monitor how much a free-fed dog is actually consuming, and if you own more than one dog, someone may be hogging all the food. Dogs don't make very good decisions about these things. Their genetic heritage has programmed them to gorge whenever food is available, and even though your Westie hasn't been living off the fat of the land for eons, his genes don't know that. Where food is concerned, he thinks he's still a wolf.

Seniors

As your Westie ages, he will becomes less active and require fewer calories. Westies are considered "seniors" at about age seven, but ten is probably more accurate. At this age, if your Westie is eating a high-quality dog food, you can safely reduce his portion. Lower-grade dog foods, however, contain just enough vitamins and minerals to keep your dog going at the amount indicated, so you will have to supplement with vitamins and minerals. Fish oil, glucosamine, chondroitin, and MSM (methylsufonylmethan) can benefit many older animals. Just check with your veterinarian before supplementing your senior Westie.

Geriatric dogs do develop special dietary needs. Unless they have kidney trouble, they need more protein than young adults, which the better commercial food manufacturers take into account. They also benefit from arginine, an essential immune-system-booster amino acid, and from omega-3 fatty acids to keep their brains and nervous system in good repair.

If your older dog continues to do well on his regular diet

Variety Is the Spice of Life

The single best thing you can do to ensure your dog is well nourished is to feed him a variety of different foods. This will not only make eating more pleasurable for him, but if you start early enough, it may help protect him from developing allergies. Provide your Westie with something besides a steady diet of commercial foods. Well-chosen, lower-fat table food can boost the quality of a meal by providing high-quality human-grade nutrients. (Rotation and variety are also important components of the ARF diet.)

Things to Avoid Feeding Your Westie

Chocolate
Chocolate, especially baker's chocolate, can cause a range of problems, including cardiovascular difficulties and even seizures.

Hoofin' It?
Cow hooves as dog treats are dangerous. They are the number one cause of tooth breakage in dogs (and they smell disgusting, to boot).

Grapes and Raisins
Reports have recently implicated large amounts of grapes and raisins (between 9 ounces and 2 pounds) in acute canine kidney failure (although no one knows exactly why). The kidney shutdown is so dramatic that aggressive treatment may be necessary to save a dog's life.

Hold the Onions
Do not feed your dog raw onions. They are potentially toxic and can cause a serious condition called Heinz-body hemolytic anemia. Ingestion of large amounts of raw or cooked onions in dogs can cause toxicity, leading to the destruction of red blood cells. This causes anemia, weakness, jaundice, bloody urine, and eventually death, one to six days after the ingestion. Don't freak out, though, if your dog eats a single onion ring. Large amounts cause the disorder, but to be prudent, shun them altogether.

Rawhide
Many Westies like rawhide chews, sometimes so much that they'll practically inhale the stuff—and the rawhide can stick in their throats. Even if your Westie gets it down, it's bleached, treated, and preserved with who-knows-what. Some are basted with flavors that can cause diarrhea. If you notice this, switch to plain rawhide treats, or—better yet—eliminate them altogether.

Salmon Poisoning Disease
The fluke *Nanophyetus salmincola* is host to a microorganism called *Neorickettsia helminthoeca* that can cause a disease commonly known as salmon poisoning disease (SPD). The organism develops in snails and infects fish, which are ingested by dogs, where they infect the intestinal tract. This microorganism is found in salmon, steelhead, trout, Pacific giant salamanders, and fresh-water fish found in and around the Pacific Ocean from northern California to Seattle, Washington. This potentially fatal disease can be prevented by not feeding your dog raw or partially cooked (or even cold-smoked) fish from this region. I avoid feeding even cooked salmon to my dogs. However, processed salmon oils as supplements do not present the same hazards.

and is not losing weight or condition, there's no reason at all to switch him. So-called senior dog foods are not required to meet any predetermined standards, so there's a fair amount of variation in formulas—read the label and select carefully if you do decide to switch.

SUPPLEMENTS AND SPECIAL DIETS

Supplements are less necessary for your dog if you're feeding a higher-quality diet. Puppies are particularly vulnerable to the dangers of oversupplementation, so don't add minerals or vitamins to your puppy's diet without a recommendation from your veterinarian.

Sometimes a medical condition can necessitate a special veterinary diet. Conventional allopathic vets will prescribe a special diet to address a dog's particular medical issue. Many people who have chosen holistic care for their Westies have

Make sure you feed your Westie age-appropriate food.

found alternative supplements, herbs, homeopathic, and other alternatives helpful in preventing problems, maintaining balance, or treating special medical conditions. But even these alternatives emphasize sound nutrition as a starting point in treatment.

OBESITY

Obesity is the number one nutritional disorder in American dogs (and American people). Sixty percent of all adult dogs in the United States are overweight. This exacerbates problems such as diabetes and arthritis, and shortens a dog's life.

Obesity is defined as being 10 to 25 percent above ideal weight. How can you tell if your Westie is overweight? Look at him from above. You should be able to see an actual waist. By running your thumbs along your dog's spine, you should be able feel each rib without putting pressure on the rib cage. When viewed from the side, his waist should be well defined—like Scarlett O'Hara's.

Most cases of obesity arise from overfeeding and underexercising. (In a few instances, a medical condition like hypothyroidism or insulin imbalance can cause the problem. Check with your veterinarian to rule out any medical issues before attempting to slim him down to "Speedo" weight.) Unless your Westie can drive to the store, fill a shopping cart with junk food, and escape without paying or setting off an alarm, you cannot blame *him* for being hefty. You're the one with the loot and the wheels. You decide what goes into his bowl and what treats to give him.

To make sure your Westie's weight stays normal, feed him a proper amount of food for his ideal weight, and exercise him—it's that easy. Your vet can advise. Try to stay away from treats, but if you do like to treat your dog, try baby carrots. If your Westie is overweight, a commercial "lite" food may help him shed unwanted blubber. Pick a high-quality formula that includes specific weight loss directions.

Most dogs don't seem to mind exercise nearly as much as most people do. A long power walk will benefit both of you. Some people take turns with their dogs on the treadmill. However, before starting any exercise or weight-loss program for your dog, consult your vet.

Treats and Bones

Most people enjoy giving their dogs treats, and as long as you don't overfeed, go for it. Read the label on any box of dog treats. There are a growing variety of nutritious dog biscuits on the market, made with health-supporting organically grown ingredients. Avoid treats that contain artificial colors, flavors, and dyes.

If your Westie is getting a bit round in the middle, replace high-calorie treats with fresh vegetables like broccoli. (My dogs go nuts for bell peppers and even artichoke leaves!) Offer your Westie raw carrots or any vegetable or fruit that he will eat.

Bones are naturally balanced sources of calcium and phosphorous that dogs practically worship. Avoid feeding cooked bones, since they easily splinter and can damage your dog's throat and digestive system. Also, forgo the sterilized bones available in stores. Their unnatural hardness can break teeth. Whole fresh bones are safer, but some people prefer to have the bones thoroughly ground.

Raw bones may carry bacterial dangers, but after personally feeding fresh raw chicken wings and necks to my dogs for years—without incident—I feel that the nutritional and dental benefits are hard to deny. It's important that the bones be both fresh and meaty. Start your dog off gradually, and watch him carefully. Supervision is important—dogs need to learn to eat bones properly.

GROOMING

YOUR WEST HIGHLAND
WHITE TERRIER

T he Westie is often classified as a "nonshedding breed." Westies have a double coat: an outer coat that consists of straight, hard white hair, and an undercoat that is short and downy with insulating properties. In its natural state, the Westie's hair needs help to "shed," usually with the help of a groomer. Otherwise it will mat and you will end up with a tangled and unhappy Westie. In the breed's indigenous Scottish Highlands, the double coat provided protection against the elements, but there were enough natural bramble and bush to "groom" him naturally.

Most Westie owners find that working with a professional groomer is the best way to keep their Westie looking good. The Westie coat does need some special attention, and many find that it's best to leave it to the professionals. Even with professional grooming, though, you'll still need to spend time brushing your Westie.

Some owners do learn to do their own grooming. They may be dissatisfied with professionals, wish to learn the skill themselves, or wish to save some money. In any case, grooming your own Westie can contribute to the bonding between the two of you. Count on making mistakes while learning, but have faith that the hair will grow out.

THE GREAT DEBATE: STRIPPER OR CLIPPER?

There are two ways to care for your Westie's coat: stripping and clipping. If you have a show Westie, the breed standard requires hand stripping, but if you are not showing your dog, it's more than likely that you will end up clipping him.

Stripping

With a stripped coat, loose, dead hairs are plucked out to leave a vibrant, healthy, and functional coat. Using a stripping knife, you hold a small amount of hair on the blade and pull dead hairs out of the coat. If you are not showing your dog, whether or not you strip (or "pluck") your pet is strictly optional.

Some advantages of stripping are that it makes your Westie's coat harsher and coarser, helps maintain its double-coated protection, and cuts down on doggy odor. On the other hand, stripping can irritate your dog (many Westie's don't like it), it's harder to find a groomer willing to strip your dog, and it's more expensive and time-consuming than clipping.

Few "garden variety" groomers are willing to strip a Westie: It takes too long, and it requires a great degree of skill to master the art (and it *is* an art). However, some breeder/exhibitors may be willing to teach you the process. Others may "moonlight" and will strip your Westie for you if you're willing to pay. You may occasionally run into a professional groomer who'll strip your Westie, but it can be expensive. There are also books and pamphlets that provide instruction on how to do it yourself.

above: *Stripping the coat involves plucking out dead hairs with a stripping knife.*

right: *Clipping the coat requires special dog clippers.*

Clipping

If you are not showing your dog, clipping your Westie will probably be your best option. Clipping, which you will probably want a professional groomer to handle, requires special dog clippers with various blade attachments. It can also involve the use of scissors. Clipping is a lot easier on the dog and far less time-consuming than stripping.

Clipping the coat discourages the growth of hard hair, and eventually the dog's coat becomes just soft undercoat. A clipped coat tends to lose pigment, but that is hardly a problem in this breed, where whiter coats are desirable. The soft coat that results from clipping will not be as dirt-repellant or water-resistant as a hard, stripped coat. However, with regular brushing, most dogs, either clipped or stripped, should remain fairly clean and odor-free.

A well-clipped Westie can look quite winsome—if you and the groomer know the look you're after. Many competent all-breed groomers can do a decent job of clipping. Most pet Westie owners are quite comfortable with a clipped dog, who—if groomed by a professional—generally requires trips to the groomer every four to eight weeks for bathing, clipping, and nail trimming.

Keeping your Westie neat doesn't have to take a lot of time, especially if you do it regularly. If you do strip him, pulling out a little hair a couple of times a week can keep things from getting out of hand. And if your dog is clipped, keep him brushed between grooming sessions.

BRUSHING

Brushing not only makes your dog look beautiful, it keeps him clean and healthy. And as for your Westie, well, he gets to be the center of attention. Brushing your Westie stimulates his skin and spreads the skin's natural oils throughout his coat. It encourages good circulation and reduces shedding. Westies are considered a low-shedding breed (there is no such thing as a nonshedding breed that has hair), and brushing helps shed the hair and prevents any mats from forming, which can be a real drag. If mats form and are allowed to remain too long they will tighten against your Westie's skin and cause irritation. (Note: Mats often hide in armpits.) Pet-supply outlets do offer special tools to detangle and break the mats.

Whether you are stripping or clipping your Westie's coat, you still need to accustom your dog to the idea of brushing between formal sessions. Initially, brushing is a strange feeling for him. Begin slowly, especially if he appears stressed or nervous. A conscientious breeder has probably done a bit of "priming" in this area—perhaps by pulling out the puppy coat before placing him with his new family.

Brushing Tools

It's important to use the proper grooming tools for the job, as follows:

- A high-quality slicker brush works well.
- A waist-high table or bench with a rubber mat for your dog to stand or lie on will make brushing more comfortable.
- A professional grooming table with an arm and a noose can be a good investment.
- Finer-coated Westies require a comb with tines that are close together, such as a flea comb, which will help reduce dead undercoat (and fleas, of course). Removing dead coat allows the skin to breathe.
- Heavy-coated Westies require hairbrushes. A brush with

round balls on the end of each bristle gets through with less resistance. Or—and this especially applies to hand-stripped terriers—a wider-toothed comb or an undercoat rake will do the trick.

- Another option for grooming/brushing is a "hybrid tool" that both pulls out the loosest dead hair and cuts some as well. These can produce very attractive and satisfactory results.

How to Brush Your Westie

Before you start, pay heed to the condition of the coat. Is it dry, or greasy? Hot spots, thickening of the skin, and other deviations from normal could indicate a problem.

To brush, place your Westie on a stable surface such as a grooming table or the floor. In nice weather, you can do it on a patio or on a deck. (You'll be providing nice building supplies for nest-building birds!) Work through the coat with a slicker brush, brushing the leg hair up and then down into place. Brush the hair of the head up to make the typical Westie "chrysanthemum" look. Follow all grooming and brushing time with a treat or a toy or some one-on-one playtime. Many dogs find the end of the session a relief—even cathartic. Don't forget to praise your dog to the skies.

How Frequently?

How often should you brush? According to longtime Westie owner Beth Widdows, brushing several times a week will help keep the coat looking good.

BATHING

A full grooming may include a bath. A bathtub or a utility sink works well. Use a nonskid mat in the tub to prevent slipping and potential injury. You might also want to buy a handheld spray nozzle. It's worth the modest investment because it makes it easier to thoroughly rinse off your Westie, which is important for preventing skin irritation.

Supplies

First gather all your supplies: shampoo, towels, skin conditioner, and a handheld dryer (if you are using one). You don't want to forget something and have to leave your soaking wet Westie in the tub. Some owners place cotton balls in

Brush your Westie several times a week to keep his coat looking good.

the ears to keep water from getting in, but because the Westie's ears are naturally pricked, they drain properly, so cotton balls aren't usually necessary.

Choose a shampoo that is specially formulated for your Westie's needs. Do not use anything else unless your vet recommends it. Because the pH levels required for dogs are different from those required for people, human shampoos are not appropriate. There are several good shampoos especially formulated for hard-coated terriers (if you're stripping), and ones that will enhance a vibrant white coat.

How to Bathe Your Westie

A Westie's bath water should be tepid. Lather the shampoo in your hands and work from the neck toward the back. Wash the feet, between the toes, under the tail, under the skirt. Gently wash the face with a washcloth and a bit of shampoo, carefully avoiding the eyes. Most important of all, after you lather, rinse thoroughly. Then rinse again. When you are sure you have rinsed off every molecule of shampoo, rinse once more! Shampoo residue is a major cause of itching.

Grooming Tip

If you have a lighter-skinned dog, leave more hair to protect the skin from burning. Your Westie lacks the melanin of a darker-skinned dog, and the skin is more prone to burn. If you have your Westie professionally groomed, tell the groomer to "leave a little extra on the top."

There are special nongreasy skin conditioners that penetrate the coat and moisturize the skin without leaving any residue. These can prevent your Westie's skin from drying out—especially if you bathe him frequently. Follow the instructions carefully. For dogs with dry, flaky skin, these conditioners can be sprayed on in between baths. However, if the flaky condition persists, seek veterinary advice: This condition may result from a thyroid function disorder that is easily treated.

After you've rinsed, towel dry. You may choose to air dry, but make sure the dog stays warm. Handheld dryers designed for dogs work well, but some human ones set on low temperature are fine to use, as long as you are extremely careful to avoid getting close to his skin. When drying, be especially cautious around the head.

How Frequently?

There is much to consider when answering this question for your particular dog. Many exhibitors and owners bathe their dogs only about three or four times a year because they believe that too many baths will dry out a Westie's skin and cause itching problems. This is especially true for hand-stripped dogs, whose coats tend to retain a particularly self-cleaning quality. If you are doing your own clipping and you keep up the work and brushing between "formal" grooming, this could work for you as well. Many Westie owners who take their dogs to a professional groomer simply follow the groomer's recommendations (often every four to six weeks) and bring him in for the bathing and grooming in one fell swoop.

More often than every four weeks may too frequent for the typical Westie; however, some people cannot tolerate the "bouquet" of a clipped dog and—for their own threshold of comfort—choose to bathe him more often. And a Westie with overactive oil glands may require more baths to keep the problem in check. For those dogs who get truly dirty, a bath is acceptable, as long as they are thoroughly dried afterward. In some cases, such as for dogs with skin problems frequent bathing with a medicated shampoo can help alleviate itching. Some contact allergies require that you bathe a dog (often with a prescribed shampoo) as many as two or three times a week during the worst of the contact allergy season.

NAIL CARE

Nail care is very important for any dog. If nails are neglected and allowed to grow too long, it can affect the conformation of the foot and cause deformity. When it comes to nail trimming, start young. If you have a puppy, handle his paws and feet gently to make him comfortable with it.

Tools

Use quality canine (not human) nail clippers, either scissor or guillotine type. Both kinds of clipper work fine, as long as you keep them sharp. Dull blades don't work, and they hurt the dog, and human nail clippers do not work well. Most groomers prefer guillotine-type clippers for their ease of use. Good scissor-type clippers are often stronger and sharper, and a little more accurate (for avoiding the quick of the nail). Some breeders simply use a metal file to keep nail growth under control.

A cordless grinding tool is wonderful, and some dogs prefer it once they get used to the noise. You get a nicely rounded result—free of sharp edges. One drawback is that this tool can overheat the nails. But by not spending too much time on each nail and by alternating, you can prevent it from getting too hot. I recently discovered that after a walk in the rain, my dogs' wet nails tend to reduce the friction that causes overheating and also softens the nails. Some people put a nylon stocking over the paw and let the nails peek through so that the grinder won't get caught in the hair of the paw.

How To Trim Your Westie's Nails

Nail clipping can be stressful, and I have known some dogs to hide even if they suspect or anticipate its prospect. Owners worry about hurting the dog, and their fear is translated to him. Try to make this experience as pleasant as possible for the dog. You'll need to control him, something that's best accomplished with a grooming table, although some people sit right on the floor or couch with their dog. You may need an assistant, especially at first, since many Westies, especially those without desensitization, abhor having their nails done and will resort to hiding or trying to distract you. Plying him with a tasty morsel may entice him, but not always. The trick is not to blow the process up in

Skunked!

A rendezvous with Pepé Le Pew is reason enough for unscheduled ablutions. Special products that remove skunk odor are available; some owners swear that a bath in tomato juice will do the job. But unless you have a hankering for a temporarily salmon-colored Westie, be sure to rinse thoroughly.

Dealing With Dirt

Most adventurous Westies will get dirty no matter how often they are bathed. Following are some ideas to keep your Westie clean between baths:

- When the dog comes in from a dig-a-thon, train him to wait at the door while you towel him dry. Keep a towel by the door handy for this purpose. Cover the furniture and put down a towel, sheet, or some other protection at the door.
- Crate him with a towel; within a half-hour to an hour, he'll shed most of the dirt! (You'll want to clean the crate later.) Westies naturally shed dirt once it has had a chance to dry. This tends to be especially true of hard-coated Westies. It never hurts to brush through to remove the rest of the dirt.

More adventurous Westies need to be bathed more often.

- Wash off your Westie's paws and skirt with a little lukewarm water. Try to make this a pleasurable experience; offer liberal treats and praise.
- To freshen him up for special occasions, use a little baking soda or even grooming chalk. Rub it in and brush it out—and presto, he's dazzling white and fresh as a lily.
- Waterless shampoos do a good job in a pinch. All you need is the shampoo—usually a foam—and a clean towel.
- Avoid perfumes. People may have resorted to the practice in medieval times to mask odors due to the scarcity of bathing opportunities, but this is the twenty-first century. Besides, many dogs (and people) may be allergic to them.

Removing Tar

Petroleum jelly works well for removing tar on the pads. Follow with a mild soap and warm water. Avoid using paint thinners or turpentine on your Westie's feet—they are far too harsh.

your own mind so that your Westie picks up on it and freaks out. (Of course, this can be prevented by getting your new puppy very used to letting you handle his feet.)

When clipping, try to avoid the quick, which is the vein that runs through the nail. If you accidentally clip the quick, it will hurt your Westie, and will bleed. You can easily see the quick on lighter nails, but if your dog has black nails, don't cut past the natural curve of the nail. If you haven't kept up the process, you must do this with extra caution, because if you don't cut often enough, the quick will tend to grow past the curve. Keep styptic powder around just in case you draw blood.

Hold one rear paw in one hand, firmly, but without squeezing. Most dogs are less fussy about their rear paws, so it's often easier to begin there. Separate the toes and clip (or grind) each nail right below the quick. If you leave any ragged edges, a touch-up with a nail file will polish the nails off nicely. If you use a grinder, you can round the edges with that. If you go down too far and reach the quick, apply some styptic powder to the nail to stem bleeding. A small pinch pressed against the cut nail will stop the bleeding. If you don't have styptic powder, a little cornstarch will do the trick. Try not to make a big deal of it, or your Westie may begin to fear getting his nails trimmed.

You'll also want to check the pads of your Westie's paws for foreign substances, tar, dirt, mats, or thorns. Trim the hair between the pads and tidy up the feet. Such maintenance can prevent infections.

How Frequently?

Trim his nails every other week or so. You may be able to get away with less often if your Westie walks a lot on hard pavement, which helps wear down the nail. But even then, it's a matter of luck. Some nails tend to grow more out than curled under—and it's the ones with the curve that benefit most from the pavement.

EAR CARE

The Westie's prick ears make him less prone to ear problems than most breeds, and often they are virtually self-cleaning. But problems can arise, such as ear infections. Many owners don't even realize their dog has an ear infection until they have to clean out the ears. So it is important that whenever you groom your Westie you check and clean his ears.

Your breeder, vet, or groomer can recommend a good ear-cleaning product. Do not use cotton swabs. Cotton balls are safe, but a swab can easily damage his ear if he doesn't remain stationary—and most Westies don't.

EYE CARE

Your Westie's eyes should be bright and shiny, reflecting his keen intelligence. Although eye problems are not pervasive in the breed, problems can occur in all dogs. So it's a good idea to keep tabs and seek veterinary advice if you detect any problems, such as any persistent discharge from your dog's eyes. If he squints or rubs his eyes, this could indicate a serious problem. If the white of the eye has a cloudy or bluish cast, it could be symptomatic of such inflammatory conditions such as iritis, a corneal ulcer, or glaucoma. Corneal abrasions can occur—one possible source being the scratch of a cat not thrilled by your Westie's attentions. Plants can also be the culprit. If your Westie acts confused and collides with people or objects, his vision could be impaired.

More common problems include plugged tear ducts, eye injuries, and dry eye. Diet, overall heath, and genetics can factor into these problems. They are not that common, and your veterinarian can help eliminate them if they do occur.

STAINING

Tear Staining

Tear staining—brownish streaks under the eyes—occasionally occurs in dogs, and can be particularly noticeable in light-colored dogs. To get rid of the staining, try the commercial products that are available through pet-supply stores and catalogs, or you can try a do-it-yourself formula: a tablespoon of hydrogen peroxide (make sure it's not old), a dash of milk of

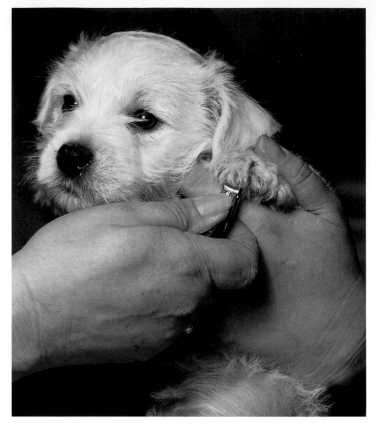

Get your Westie used to nail trimming at an early age.

magnesia, and sufficient cornstarch to form a paste. Apply the mixture to the stain—careful to avoid getting any into your Westie's eyes. After it has a little time to set and dry, rinse thoroughly. Soon the stains will disappear or at least diminish.

Tear-stain removers are just a temporary solution; they don't fix the problem. However, a change in diet to a higher-quality commercial food, home-prepared, or appropriate raw diet can correct the problem. Low-quality food that contains beet pulp may cause your Westie's eyes to run. Also, tear staining may indicate a problem that should be investigated by a vet.

Muzzle, Beard, and Paw Staining

Muzzle, beard, and paw stains may be reddish brown to burgundy in hue. Several factors are suspected of causing this condition, but saliva is the most common cause. If your dog licks a lot, staining is likely. It can happen wherever he licks his own coat, usually on the paws and muzzle. Soft coats are more prone to staining than harder ones.

So what causes the licking? Suspects include the following:
- fungi and yeast infections
- allergies with food and inhalant origins
- long hair on pads that causes objects (some as tiny as a mustard seed) to lodge in paws
- cuts and abrasions

Hair that's white at the base and that becomes stained at the top indicates that licking is the issue. Hair stained down to the base indicates that the hair is growing in stained and more likely to be of a fungal origin. If this is the case, your veterinarian can provide fungicides or treatments.

If the problem is not an infection, there are some things you might try to tackle the problem yourself. Trim the pad-hair as short as possible. This may reveal hidden objects. You might also try dipping paws in either hydrogen peroxide or a half-and-half solution of bleach and water. Rinse either off after a minute or so. The peroxide and bleach should be used sparingly since they are quite drying to the skin. You can also mix Epsom salts and strong salt water. You needn't rinse these off and you can use these more frequently. Westie breeder/handler Dee Hanna uses a formula of one-third chalk, one-third milk of magnesia, and one-third 20-percent-strength hydrogen peroxide.

If your dog's muzzle is stained, you can dip a cotton ball in fresh hydrogen peroxide and wipe the beard daily. At first the stain may turn pink, but eventually it should begin to whiten until new growth replaces the old. When the new hair grows in unstained, continue to use this as part of your maintenance grooming. If the muzzle stains are directly related to the licking problem, they, too, will likely disappear. Often the staining on the muzzle is directly related to the issue in the paws that has caused the licking, and will begin to grow out when the issue is resolved.

If the muzzle, but not the paws, is stained, look for other causes and remedies. Is red dye or beets contained in your Westie's commercial dog food? This can cause staining. Check treats also. Tomato-based spaghetti sauce will stain both human and Westie beards. (You might select an Alfredo or a white clam sauce instead of a marinara if you're planning to share an Italian dinner with him.) Water with high iron concentrations may be the culprit and might warrant a switch to bottled—or at least filtered—water. Some Westie people swear by Ester C as a preventative and antidote to staining.

DENTAL CARE

Like people, dogs are susceptible to plaque, tartar, and gum disease, which arise from the combination of food, saliva, bacteria, and cells in the mouth lining. When tartar forms on the teeth, it provides a base for more plaque to accumulate. Unless controlled, it progresses to the point of dental problems and gum disease. Since canine periodontal problems can cause myriads of other problems, prevention is key. Infections that start in the gums can migrate to other parts of the body and cause disease.

The good news is that much of this is preventable. Fortunately Westies are less likely to develop dental caries (cavities) than people are. Although it's not common for dogs to get cavities, don't tempt fate by feeding gobs of saltwater taffy and peanut brittle, because when cavities do appear in dogs, the culprit is usually a diet high in sugar content and poor preventative dental care. Brushing, a good diet, and appropriate chews can all help your Westie's teeth stay strong.

Supplies

Toothbrushes specifically made for dogs are available at pet-supply stores. Finger brushes are another option, but the toothbrush's stronger bristles are more effective at getting below the gum line, where plaque causes problems. Some dogs will tolerate electric toothbrushes, but don't count on it—the noise can be disconcerting.

Many owners brush their Westies' teeth regularly with specially formulated toothpastes flavored with beef and chicken. From their reactions, you'd think the dogs had found ambrosia (or "the food of the dogs," at least). Keep in mind that human toothpaste is inappropriate for dogs.

Brushing Your Westie's Teeth

Brushing is a good way to take inventory for broken teeth, tartar control, or any unusual changes. It also removes plaque both above and below the gum line, so concentrate the effort on those areas that dental chews and other aids do not reach. Another benefit of brushing the teeth is that it can minimize "doggie breath." If you start the brushing routine while your Westie is young, he may even look forward to it.

Start at a time when both you and your Westie are relaxed, and ease yourselves into the process. At first, don't even use a toothbrush. Hold him as if you're cuddling him and gently stroke the outside of his cheek with your finger. As he mellows out, place a dab of dog-appropriate toothpaste on your finger and allow him to sample it. (Most dogs are crazy about it.) With a tiny bit of toothpaste on the brush, gently use it on one or two teeth and on the gum line. This step accustoms your Westie to the feel of the brush. Over the next several days, gradually increase the number of teeth. Eventually brush the rear teeth; this is where plaque tends to accumulate most. Be slow and gentle, and stop before he begins to get restless. This technique establishes that it is *you* who determines when you stop, not *him*. Increase to about 30 seconds per side, concentrating on the outer tooth surfaces, since little tartar accumulates on the inner ones. Conclude each session while it is still fun, and praise your dog profusely so that your Westie will look forward to toothbrushing as an incredibly *fun* activity.

Some human plaque-attacking mouthwashes, applied with a gauze pad and wiped across the teeth, are considered safe. Your vet may stock special canine oral rinses that can be helpful. Some owners say that the tartar just slides off. Special veterinary mouthwashes can also be effective. Additionally, you can now buy little pop-up cloths that contain baking soda. The slight abrasiveness of the baking soda can help remove plaque. Other over-the-counter dental wipes found in pet-supply stores are infused with antiplaque ingredients. New products, including a gel that you can rub on your dog's teeth and gum line, kill plaque-causing bacteria and have even proven to reverse gingivitis. There is also a safe water additive that can aid in dental hygiene.

How Frequently?

In a perfect world, you would brush your Westie's teeth as frequently as you do your own. But if a daily routine just isn't possible, try for at least three times a week. Your Westie's mouth will benefit enormously from it.

Diet and Dental Health

Many vets and breeders have found that feeding a hard kibble diet can slightly reduce your dog's chances of developing dental problems. Some vets recommend special kibbles formulated for tartar control. Certain veterinary rawhide chews infused with enzymes may prevent plaque accumulation and are popular with many dog owners.

Some Appropriate Raw Food (ARF) adherents testify that their dogs' teeth and gums are so healthy that they've never required professional dental cleanings, since some of the diet's staples, which include raw chicken wings and necks, do double-duty as nutrition and dentifrice. The natural enzymes in these foods have proven effective in maintaining excellent tooth and gum health.

For those who choose to follow a more conventional feeding regime, offering your Westie a human-quality raw bone periodically can do wonders to help stave off the dental and

Chew Tips

- Rawhide chews help to clean the teeth; however, great care should be exercised when using rawhide products. Westies can choke on large pieces of rawhide, and they can become lodged in the throat, causing choking.
- Dental chew toys made of nylon and hard knobby rubber satisfy a Westie's desire for chewing and help support dental health. Another benefit is that they are virtually indestructible.

Dental care is essential for your Westie's health.

If you are showing your Westie, you will probably end up seeking out a professional groomer.

periodontal disease that can compromise his health. Some Westie owners offer their dogs a raw buffalo or beef bone every couple of weeks to naturally maintain their dogs' dental health. The head of the femur bones are primo because the gristle functions much like the bristles of a toothbrush.

Professional Cleaning

Many dogs need to have regular dental cleanings under anesthesia. But regular preventative dental care can save you money in the long run and keep dental cleanings and extractions over the years to a minimum.

A professional cleaning entails anesthesia, a thorough flushing of the mouth, and the use of ultrasonic scalers and other instruments to remove all tartar. The vet will also polish the teeth to help eliminate the little pits or scratches that plaque likes to call home. It sure beats deterioration, which would make your Westie a candidate for dental implants and da Vinci porcelain veneers à la *Extreme Makeover* (Terrier Version).

PROFESSIONAL GROOMING

Some Westie owners handle all of their dogs' grooming needs at home, but some prefer to go the route of the professional groomer. If do you choose to use a professional groomer, start getting your Westie used to it at a young age. After the puppy has had all his shots—at about 14 weeks—make an appointment for a "puppy cut" (a modified, less-time-consuming version of the adult cut) to expose him to the grooming experience while he's still in a spongelike learning stage. If the groomer has the right touch, the puppy will discover that it's a pleasant experience, and he will come to accept grooming as "just another trip to the beauty salon." After a few appointments, ask the groomer to give him a "Westie cut." The groomer may know exactly what you mean, but just in case bring along a photo of how you would like your Westie to look (presumably, like a Westie). Politely and clearly insist that you do not want your Westie to resemble a Schnauzer or a Scottie. The modern Westie looks quite tailored. The groomer needs to know that the Westie has a round head, a carrot tail, and a skirt blended without obvious lines. This takes more time, but by that point, your Westie should be perfectly OK with it.

Finding a Groomer

Interview the groomer before the first appointment. Ask about the process. Does he or she use a drying cage? If so, is it an open crate? The open crate is safer than the enclosed ones some groomers use. Will your dog be attended to when he's noosed and on the grooming table? Does the groomer express anal glands as part of the routine? If so, you may wish to opt out, since this is rarely necessary in Westies; so let the groomer know and remind him or her each time until he or she gets the idea. If the groomer balks at any of your questions or requests, or acts rude, find another groomer. If you cannot find a good groomer in your area, contact your local Westie club to see if any members have their dogs groomed in your neighborhood.

If you choose to use a groomer, you might have to leave your dog for several hours. Some days tend to be busier than others, so arrange an appointment according to your preferences. If you want your dog back sooner, you might ask which days are slowest. Perhaps, if you have some free time, you can hang out in the waiting area and read the newspaper or a novel. Sometimes the extra time is just what you need to regroup, get a cup of coffee, or accomplish an errand or two. If you have to work or require more time, your Westie should be able to remain at the shop a bit longer.

Fighting Doggie Bad Breath

Good preventative dental care will do much to minimize canine halitosis. But there are other ways to address this problem. Christine Swingle, a breeder for more than forty years, offers her Westies fresh mint leaves, which they seem to enjoy. And I have been known to slip my dogs the occasional peppermint breath mint every now and again.

Although it's most likely to be caused by a dental problem, bad breath can arise from other organic problems such as diabetes, kidney disease, gastrointestinal issues, respiratory problems—and even tonsillitis. Of course, a temporary dalliance with this problem may have to do with his "choice of cuisine." If you're the proud owner of a Westie who enjoys recycling poop, this could explain a lot. There is no accounting for taste.

TRAINING AND BEHAVIOR

OF YOUR WEST
HIGHLAND WHITE TERRIER

On the continuum of purebred dogs, Westies are considered moderately obedient. Generally a person will not say, "Gee, I want an obedience dog—I'm getting a Westie." A Westie can be compliant, but in the pool of multiple intelligences, he will rate higher in areas of independent problem solving than he will in rote learning or obsequiousness. He wants to please, but he was bred to be a working dog—and part of that incorporates his naturally high prey drive and his desire to rid the universe of all vermin.

Even so, it's a myth that you cannot train a Westie. (There are even some obedience judges who believe that using the words *terrier* and *obedience* in the same sentence is oxymoronic!) With your patience, consistency, and positive training, your Westie can be well trained, as long as you keep things interesting and mentally stimulating for him. What fun it is to attend an obedience trial and watch the only Westie in the ring blow away his competition, including Border Collies, Golden Retrievers, and other so-called obedience breeds!

TRAINING STARTS EARLY

Whether your ultimate goal is competitive obedience or simple puppy socialization and household manners, training really does begin in the whelping box very soon after birth. Each puppy, through social interaction, learns from the very beginning about positive and negative experiences. First, their mother provides them with warmth, food, and physical stimulation. She washes them with her tongue and her licking helps them eliminate, after which she cleans up. If all goes well, they begin to see life as something enjoyable.

In the litter, puppies socialize each other. They react to the force of each other's mouthing and biting, and if it's too severe, the perpetrator will get an unequivocal message (a yelp). They begin to work out their hierarchy; though theoretically much of it is imprinted and only needs to emerge and be sorted out in these tiny beings' growing world.

The earlier you start training, the better. When starting with a younger dog, you have fewer reinforced bad habits to overcome.

THE IMPORTANCE OF SOCIALIZATION

A responsible and canny breeder, as well as a puppy's dam and his littermates, will initiate and supervise a puppy's early socialization. You can continue to socialize your Westie when you bring him into his new home.

If your Westie puppy is between 4 and 12 months, he's in his main socialization period. It's his opportunity to learn how to interact appropriately with others and respond positively to training. Take advantage of this period to ensure his development into a happy and confident member of your family.

Around the middle of this period is the so-called "fear period." This corresponds to a similar time for pups or wolf cubs in the wild, who would first leave their dens to meet the world—a world full of dangers, so that the puppies were programmed to act with caution for survival. Today, those same instincts remain intact, so it's essential that during this period your puppy have as few fearful experiences as possible to prevent them from becoming instilled in his psyche.

Gradually introduce him to new things; let him meet other dogs and people a few at a time. Avoid immersing him into a large group of strangers. You know your puppy best, so try to gauge his readiness to expand his world. Puppy kindergartens, playgroups, friends' houses, and pet-supply stores are appropriate initiations, as long as the experiences are kept positive.

As his confidence grows, introduce him—in a positive way—to nail clippers, the vacuum cleaner, and other noisy appliances. He will learn that raucous sounds don't necessarily mean pain, and his self-assurance will grow.

Take him on walks to meet people of all ages, races, dress, and size. Expose him slowly to people in wheelchairs, people with canes, and people using walkers. Have him make friends with babies, children, people in uniform, men with beards, people with purple hair, tattoos, and funny hats. Getting used to many different types of people and things in a positive way will help him from becoming a fearful dog.

CRATE TRAINING

Few things you will acquire for your Westie will be more useful than a crate. To the novice dog owner, the crate is often misunderstood. It's not a prison; it's an essential basic item for any new puppy or dog. In reality, this multipurpose, inexpensive item combines security, a hang-out, travel safety, a time-out room, a housetraining tool, and a shelter. It will protect your puppy and your house when you cannot be home with him. No dog owner should be without one.

The safest mode of transportation for your Westie is your crate or carrier. Secured in a vehicle (bungee cords and seatbelts work well together), crates have saved thousands of dogs' lives. Furthermore, your dog will associate it with adventure, travel, and being with you—his very favorite person.

Used judiciously, a crate is an "inanimate babysitter." When you step out for a while, it keeps your dog safe and out of mischief. After a dog's surgery or injury, veterinarians often recommend crate rest, and with a terrier—who's curious and doesn't like to be kept down—you will ooze with gratitude that you have such a versatile and wonderful tool. And of course, housetraining becomes a snap.

Size and Type

Crates come in a variety of styles and are made from an assortment of materials—from straight wire to plastic and metal. You can even buy a furniture-grade solid-oak version, sure to

become a cherished antique and heirloom in years to come.

Making a den is a natural urge for a dog, harking back to his wolfish roots for safety and refuge. It should not be palatial, but the crate needs to be wide enough for your Westie pup to stand up, turn around, and lie down in comfortably. Some Westie owners start with a smaller crate, graduating to a larger one as the puppy reaches full size. The advantage to that is that a dog will rarely, if ever, soil his own living quarters. Another option is to purchase a larger crate and partition off a section of it, so that the actual space the dog uses is reduced. As your Westie grows, you can adjust the size of the crate by increasing its usable space.

Be sure to socialize your Westie with other friendly dogs.

Location

Place the crate in a central location—where there is some activity, but not so busy that it's like Grand Central Station. You want him to be relatively calm, but you also want him to become used to being a part of his human family. You might choose to place the crate in your bedroom, so the puppy feels more secure. Avoid placing it near drafts or heaters, and make it comfy and fun with a soft blanket or a crate pad and a soft toy or safe chew toy.

How to Crate Train

Here's how to acclimate your dog to a crate:

- Choose a location for the crate.
- Tell your puppy to get into his crate—you can throw a treat in the back to make him more interested. Shut the door, treat him, and praise him highly. Repeat this process again and again, leaving him in for just a few minutes at a time.
- Increase your puppy's time in the crate to five minutes, but do not leave the room—quietly remain within sight. Gradually increase this time.
- Next, leave the room while your dog is in the crate (filled with his assortment of goodies). Start with a few minutes and gradually work your way up to longer times.
- Always have the crate out and available for your Westie. When he is out and about, leave the door open, and you will notice that he will begin to retreat to it by his own volition.
- Give him a toy or snack to occupy him and help him associate the crate with marvelous things. Try filling a toy with peanut butter or spray cheese.

A crate can be a haven that, when filled with his cherished objects, reinforces your Westie's security. Feeding a dog in the crate and giving him special treats will make it all the more enticing. Eventually your Westie *will* go to his crate of his own volition. And every time he does, effusively praise and treat!

How Long?

Forcing a dog to stay in a crate too long defeats the very purpose of crate training. After all, he can only hold it so long, and if left in a crate for an extended period of time, your poor Westie will be forced to urinate in it. This in turn breaks down the natural inhibitions he has about converting his boudoir into a bathroom. And it just goes downhill from there.

The common lore is that a puppy up to eight months old can control his bladder for as many hours as his age in months, plus one. Ergo, a two-month-old puppy should be continent for three hours. However, puppies need plenty of exercise and opportunity to explore their environment, so crating an eight-month-old dog all day is cruel. Even if he manages to develop the bladder of a camel, overcrating could predispose him to bladder stones.

Four hours is a good maximum, because it's important to heed your Westie's psychological and exercise needs. He will not appreciate the sensory deprivation that comes with long periods of solitary confinement. (Of course, at night—if you're lucky—he'll eventually sleep for longer than four hours!)

If crating your Westie for longer periods is inevitable, exercise him liberally before and after—even if this means getting up at the crack of dawn. If your schedule forces you to leave him much longer, hire a dog walker to attend to his needs.

HOLD THAT THOUGHT: HOUSETRAINING YOUR WESTIE

Westies are very intelligent, and most are easily housetrained. However, well-bred and socialized pups raised by an attentive mother and given clean living quarters tend have a leg up when it comes to housetraining.

Getting Started

Set up a schedule for taking your Westie out for potty breaks. After all, preventing mistakes is much easier than correcting them. Take your Westie puppy out before he has a chance to have an accident. Natural times include immediately after a nap, in the morning, after a vigorous play session, and after meals. Also, keep a close eye on him—he will cue you that he has to go out whenever he begins to sniff the ground or walk in circles. You may want to have a simultaneous command like "go" or "hurry up" that he associates with using the potty. After he eliminates, praise him profusely! You want him to think he has done something incredibly important, like won the Nobel Prize or the lottery jackpot.

A crate can be a haven that reinforces your Westie's feeling of security.

Using the Crate for Housetraining

Restrict your dog from having full run of the house until he is reliable. If he's having accidents, he is not ready for unrestricted freedom. This is where the crate comes in handy. If you're too busy or preoccupied to watch him like a hawk, place him in his crate—remember, it should be no larger than he needs in order to stand up, turn around, and

lie down. If you use a larger crate, you can insert a barrier to make the usable area smaller. When you remove your puppy from the crate to go potty and he doesn't go, replace him in the crate for another 15 minutes or so before trying again—you may need to repeat this several times, but eventually, nature will prevail, your Westie will eliminate, and then you can praise him like there's no tomorrow!

Accidents Will Happen

You can turn an almost-miss into a hit. It is merely opportunity knocking if you catch your Westie pup starting to potty in the house. You have just been awarded a bonus occasion to enforce desired behavior. This requires good reflexes and absolute vigilance. You can startle him with a sharp "No," quickly scoop him up, change your tone to a cheerful, jovial, "Let's go outside," and hightail it out the door to puppy's latrine area. Then place the puppy there, and give him his command to go. Be consistent and always use the same command. Let him finish, and once again lavish him with praise for his stellar accomplishment. If he doesn't oblige, it's back to the crate again. Repeat as necessary.

Punishment Doesn't Work

A missed opportunity is just that—a missed opportunity. This is true even if you scold your puppy five seconds after he's eliminated on your expensive Persian rug. (Wait! What were you thinking, taking an unreliable puppy into that room with a priceless rug?) Young puppies live in the "here and now" and really do have the retention ability of only about five seconds. Moreover, you should blame yourself for not supervising closely. (But don't forget to forgive yourself soon.) Just vow to be more alert next time.

Cleaning Up Accidents

Dogs are olfactory wonders; they can smell a million things that you cannot. If your dog smells remnants of urine or feces, it's as if he's received an invitation from a best friend to join the party and add more "fun." So it's important to immediately clean up any area where he's just had an accident. Special enzymatic cleaners, available at pet-supply stores, neutralize the odor. These really do work.

Vinegar may work for linoleum and other hard, nonabsorbent floorings. But it only really works on carpets if you don't mind the aroma of dog "piss and vinegar." It does not remove dog-urine odors from carpet. Avoid using ammonia-based cleaners to remove a dog urine stain. Since ammonia smells like urine to a dog, you'll only succeed in "indicating the restroom."

Patience and consistency are essential for housetraining.

Scolding a dog by rubbing his nose in his urine may allow you to vent your own frustration, but it will do nothing to help your pup get the message. (One dog owner opines that this sort of punishment might actually cause the puppy to start "eating the evidence" himself. Then you'll have but two nasty habits with which to wrestle.) If you yell and punish for housetraining accidents, your Westie will have no idea why you are upset with him.

The process of housetraining your Westie can be frustrating and tiring at times, but it's worth it. Hang in there, be patient, and don't give up. With consistency and patience you will prevail over his "spontaneous nature." Remember that most dogs eventually become housetrained—just like kids.

TRAINING YOUR WESTIE

Whether you're just aiming for a well-mannered Westie or preparing for formal obedience competition, it's a good idea to enroll your Westie in a beginning obedience class. Dog obedience clubs, community schools, and dog training schools offer classes.

Puppy kindergartens offer opportunities for socialization (for both dogs and owners), basic canine etiquette (such as not jumping on people), and further bonding between you and your Westie. You'll get the most out of these classes if you not only attend them regularly but also practice what you've learned and encourage other family members to do so, too. Puppies assimilate information quickly; "you can't teach an old dog new tricks" is more myth than reality. Dogs are lifelong learners.

Finding a Trainer

Ask your vet, other Westie owners, your breeder, or your breed club for recommendations. You can also check out the Association of Pet Dog Trainers (APDT), which lists approved instructors on their website (www.apdt.com).

Interview prospective obedience instructors and observe their methods. If possible, observe a class and talk to the instructor and students. If the dogs and handlers seem happy and working well together, it's a good sign. An instructor who understands and appreciates that special, plucky, confident, and often vocal terrier personality—and knows what motivates terriers—will recognize that they can do very well in obedience.

Opinions on training methods vary according to instructor and by degrees; to choose correctly for your dog or your situation, carefully evaluate all the variables. Trust your heart and cue into your Westie for clues. With the help of a competent instructor with whom both you and the dog have a rapport, you'll figure out the most suitable approach for your dog. And if you're not getting the results you want, try another trainer.

At-Home Training

Your Westie will respond well to the mutual trust that comes with positive, reward-based training. Positive training may not be the fastest way to get the results you want, but

because it builds rather than damages your relationship, it is the most satisfying method. Establishing trust and creating a safe environment pay off in spades. Praise is always preferable to punishment, and training is essentially teaching.

These days the prevailing philosophy on dog training focuses on positive, reward-based training, but this has not always been the case. In the past, the aim was to get your dog to behave through commands and correction. The "reward" was that your dog would not have to suffer the constant yank on the collar. Though these practices often resulted in a compliant dog, they often came at the expense of a happy attitude and a dog/owner bond that mutual respect fosters.

Like a child, a puppy thrives in an environment with generous measures of both consistency and love. Such an environment works miracles. Your Westie probably wants to please you, so if you communicate your limits clearly, he will gladly cooperate. Terriers, in particular, do not suffer nagging and punishment that they don't understand with grace. A rebellious Westie is like the teenager from Hades!

Mix it up!

Repetition bores a Westie, so mix your training up a bit. A Westie who knows he's loved is not lacking in self-confidence. Sure, he likes praise, but Westies are not considered a needy or clingy breed. Training that remains fun will motivate your Westie.

Decide what you really want your Westie to learn, and advance step-by-step, building new skills upon older ones. What motivates him most? Food is usually a good bet. But there are some Westies who will go wild for a toy or would sell their own mothers for a ratty tennis ball. Praise will reinforce him, but few terriers live for praise alone. They're negotiators by nature. However, each Westie is an individual, and you need to discover whatever it is that "floats his boat."

While dogs (and especially Westies) can develop pretty extensive passive vocabularies, they are more attuned to your tone of voice than to your words. Tone should match meaning. Praising your dog in a gruff or lackluster tone of voice won't convey the message, just as scolding him in a voice and tone radiating sweetness and light is apt to bewilder him.

Just like in stand-up comedy, in training, timing is everything. Reward desirable behavior the instant it occurs—not one minute later. Westies are better than we are at living in the moment.

Though some Westies will do anything for a favorite toy, many are food-crazy. Good edible rewards include string cheese, natural meat jerky, and raw vegetable morsels—all cut into very small pieces. You might want to try visiting an Asian grocery store and buying a bag of dried anchovies. This healthy snack is inexpensive, neat, and great for a Westie's skin and coat.

If weight control is an issue and you are feeding a kibble, reserve a small amount of the day's quota for training. Or if you're as lucky as I am, your terrier will work for lettuce (romaine, naturally—no iceberg, if you please).

BASIC COMMANDS

All training commands make use of treats, bait, incentives—all different names for the same thing. When you are first teaching a new skill, use a treat every time. As your

Westie learns to respond to your commands, start doling out treats intermittently. Once animals understand what you require of them, they actually learn better this way.

Training should be gentle and noncoercive. If your Westie breaks any of the commands too quickly, simply refrain from rewarding him. He needs to learn that he receives a treat only when he has completed and held the command.

Sit

This is probably the easiest command to teach your puppy. Grab a few treats. Then, holding a treat at your puppy's nose level, move your hand slowly over toward the top of his head and say, "Sit." Most puppies will automatically move into a sit in order to retrieve the treat. Reward him the instant he sits, and lay the praise on thickly. Practice this several times, but don't overdo it. Do not force him into the sit; encouragement and rewards alone will work.

Hold a small treat at your Westie's nose, then move it above his head to get him to sit.

Teach your puppy to sit before he eats, before he goes out the door, or before any exciting activity. This will give him an opportunity to chill out, and give you the chance to maintain control over his behavior.

Down

Most dogs would rather lie down on their own volition than be told to do so. This is because the "down" position puts them in a physically and psychologically vulnerable place. Just the same, you'll want to teach your Westie this command.

Start with a treat in your hand. While the dog is sitting, lower the treat slowly, moving it between his front legs, toward the floor, and using the command "down." Most dogs will lie down naturally. If after a few tries, your Westie refuses, gently extend his front legs and ease him to the floor, praising him all the time. Practice a few times; he should soon oblige. Avoid forcing him down, so that he doesn't associate this command with fear or discomfort.

Stay

This command can literally save your dog's life. It can prevent him from bolting out the front door into a busy, dangerous street. It can also calm him down in a potentially stressful situation such as a visit to the vet's office. An extension of the sit command—if you teach him to hold his sit until you release him—the stay command is a natural outgrowth. Ask your dog to sit, then intermittently reinforce his position with praise and treats and repeat, "Stay." Over time, you can slowly extend the time. You can use the same method to solidify the down command into a down-stay command.

Come

Teaching your Westie to come on command is one of the most important lessons of all. Like the stay command, the come command can save your dog's life. It reinforces the behavior that causes your dog to check in with you. Through this you gain enough control that he looks to you for security. If he's keyed in to you, he'll be more attracted to coming when called—to the one he loves and trusts most—than he will to potentially perilous situations.

While this command is extremely important, it can be the most difficult to teach. Your Westie's independent nature runs contrary to coming when called, but with your patience, he will learn. If you provide him with a good incentive to come, he will be more likely to happily oblige. It helps that he is learning that you are the source of treats, praise, and many worthwhile things. The cardinal rule is to avoid ever calling your Westie when you plan to do something he might not want to do—like taking a bath or getting a nail trim.

Start in your fenced yard and start as young as possible, when your dog is more dependent on you. First, move away from him, then encourage him to follow by calling softly to him. Dogs, especially terriers, can see a moving target more clearly than a stationary one. He will probably follow you, but keep a leash on him for all the early lessons. If he starts to run away, don't chase him; he'll see this reaction as an invitation to a game of "keep away."

You can also start inside, in a small room. Call him gently, proffering a treat. As he toddles over to you, give him the treat and shower him with praise. If he doesn't come, gently and encouragingly draw his leash toward you, taking care not to jerk on it. This is important—the leash is there to help him focus. As soon as he heads toward you, pour on the praise, and when he reaches you, treat him. Kneeling to his level will give a reluctant dog confidence. Lean back with open arms as you call him. This inviting gesture usually elicits the desired response.

Practice this three or four times a day, but only when the environment is calm and free from distractions. If your Westie is unable to concentrate, failure is guaranteed. In essence, in order to get him to come to you in the beginning, you need to be the most interesting thing in his world.

Leave It

Dogs are forever getting into garbage, pantries, and underwear drawers. In order to get yours to stop chewing something valuable, or to put down something dangerous he's picked up, teach him the leave it command.

Wait until he begins halfheartedly chewing on an object (hopefully not a family heirloom). As he's chewing, approach him, and say, "Leave it!" Trade him the object for something more toothsome, and praise him when he accepts the exchange.

This command is especially useful in real-life situations. A normal Westie will not voluntarily trade a filet mignon for a dried-out old dog biscuit, but he can—with persistence and reinforcement—learn to do so (albeit reluctantly). When he does, reward him with a jar of caviar.

Stand

"Stand" is an especially useful command. Dogs stand while they are being bathed, groomed, and examined by the vet; show dogs stand in the show ring. To teach this command, get some treats. Slowly raise one to the point where his nose would be if he were standing and say, "Stand." Before you know it, with your firm command, your Westie will stand. Reinforce this with food or a favorite game or toy.

Leash Training

Westies can be pullers, so it's important for your dog to learn to walk calmly and pleasantly on a leash. Think of this as a way to stay close to your dog. After all, your Westie will antic-

Reward your Westie with a small treat when he performs the proper command.

ipate fresh air, sunshine, and scoping the hood, because a leash means that it is time for a walk! If you don't master this very early, get used to everyone on the block asking you, "Who's walking whom?"

To get your Westie used to his leash, attach it to his collar and let him drag it around the house. Make sure you supervise him the entire time, so he doesn't accidentally get the leash caught on something and end up hurting himself. He may balk a bit at first, but soon he will forget the leash is there. After a few minutes, gently pick up the end of the leash and follow your dog. Hold the leash end, call him toward you, then praise and treat him. Continue enticing him with treats. If he resists, don't tug; just remain stationary and call him again, tasty morsel in hand. Keeping the sessions short and fun will allow him to catch on quickly. Westies are quick studies, especially if there's something in it for them.

PROBLEM BEHAVIORS

Dogs will exhibit problem behaviors for a variety of reasons. Boredom, loneliness, and pent-up energy can result in destructive chewing, nuisance barking, and ignoring limits or guidance from their owners. So-called aggressive behaviors can result from a lack of bite-inhibition training or even from fear. Though domesticated, dogs are predators. Without appropriate outlets, they may chase, stalk, bite, and destroy. They're also—and this is especially true of terriers—pack animals, so isolation can result in scratching, digging, chewing, or melancholy (and often annoying) vocalization. Essentially, they misbehave because they have no idea who's the boss! Our tendency to anthropomorphize dogs only widens the communication gap between our two species.

Just because a Westie is a small dog doesn't mean he isn't equipped with large teeth and a powerful jaw, so it is important to address any issues that might put him, yourself, or anyone else at risk. Do not hesitate to seek professional help for any problem that you cannot handle yourself.

Much of the information in the following sections is based on the philosophies, advice, and writings of Westie owner, trainer, author, and canine behaviorist, Deb Duncan (www.thedogspeaks.com).

Barking

"Barking is a major aspect of a dog's communication system," says Duncan. "They bark to alert their pack of possible danger and to warn off perceived interlopers or predators." They also bark during play, to initiate play, in response to another dog's barking, to communicate a need, to get your attention ("feed me!"), or just to let off steam. An instinctual trigger, such as a squirrel in the yard can cause barking. Many dogs bark out of unmitigated boredom.

Duncan notes that when dogs bark, most people yell to stop the barking. Not only will this not work, it will exacerbate the situation. A dog's hearing is extremely acute, so when we yell, our voices sound distorted to his ultra-acute hearing—distorted to the point that any speech is incomprehensible. When loud sounds disturb us—for instance, when a commercial comes on during a television show—we rush to turn down the volume. He cannot do that. So if we shout at the dog, we actually produce what he perceives as cacophony! To him, we might as well be another barking dog. Consider the chain reaction among dogs when one dog begins to bark. When we yell, we perpetuate a barking frenzy between ourselves and our dog, which escalates the very behavior we wish to eradicate.

Your overexcitement and extreme physical body language will fuel your dog's already heightened emotional state and reinforce his barking. If your dog's barks are reactions to the doorbell, your desperate efforts to quiet him (or even incarcerate him) will only exacerbate the problem—especially if you, too, are freaking out. Your dog is probably thinking of the situation as a version of *Let's Make a Deal*. What's behind the door—a side of corn-fed organic beef or a dognapper hired by Cruella de Ville?

Modify your dog's barking by remaining unruffled. Duncan advises getting the dog's attention by calmly approaching him, raising his head so he looks at you, and telling him, "No bark" in a firm but controlled tone of voice. Verbally reinforce his behavior the second he stops bark-

ing ("Good 'no bark'!"). Then redirect his attention away from whatever set off his barking by using a toy, a treat, a command like sit, or whatever else works.

Be consistent, patient, and understanding. Dogs learn desirable behaviors through "patterning." "This is especially true if the behavior contradicts the dog's basic nature," Duncan emphasizes. Find a way to reinforce the new positive behavior even when you're not around. Since barking is "self-reinforcing," the last thing you want is for your dog to engage in unchecked barking. Successfully deter this by restricting him from a particular area—blocking his view of, for instance, the neighborhood cat, whose sole purpose in life is to sun herself in your driveway while teasing your Westie. During the time you are "patterning" new behaviors to those triggers, Duncan suggests masking outside sounds that may provoke your dog to react, by using alternate sounds. Mozart played in a continuous loop will not only camouflage a reaction-provoking auditory catalyst, it might add a few points to your Westie's already high IQ. If you're using the television for this purpose, a TV show featuring rodents may not be the best choice, but an all-news channel may be sufficiently nontriggering (unless your Westie has a manic interest in the workings of the US Congress).

Puppies love to chew, so be sure to provide your Westie with appropriate chew toys.

Duncan stresses that your efforts require consistency, patience, and understanding—especially since you are asking your dog to behave in a manner that contradicts his instincts. How you handle his behaviors will either support or thwart your desired results as well as your relationship. So it is essential to remain positive. Take the time to understand and realize the whys and wherefores of your Westie's behavior; your reactions do impact his emotional state.

Chewing

Deb Duncan affirms that puppies will chew, and so will older dogs never taught not to. They chew because it is natural, and when they are teething, chewing gives them physical relief. Like a teething infant, a puppy needs teething toys, too—or he will, out of sheer desperation, chew on practically everything not nailed down—just to alleviate the pain of new teeth breaking through the gums.

Provide your Westie with plenty of chew toys. Keep all "enticing" no-no items out of his reach until he learns the difference between what's acceptable to chew and what's not. (It's not his fault if he destroys, beyond recognition, the favorite pair of sandals that you left on the floor.)

Products made of bitter apple, available in both spray and cream formulas, may help deter your Westie puppy from destroying your possessions. The spray is safe to use on most items. Use the cream on the antique furniture, cabinets, moldings, and on metal items. Reapply it regularly, as it loses its potency quickly. Also hope that your dog doesn't acquire a taste for the stuff (like one of mine did).

To correct puppies and older dogs not previously taught "chewing etiquette," Duncan recommends catching them in the act. Scolding them after the fact merely perplexes them. So if your dog appears penitent or looks guilty, it's in reaction to your current disapproval. A shake can is an effective distraction for inappropriate chewing. Shake the can and say, "No chew; good no chew," and immediately shift his attention to a permissible chew toy. Then play with him for a few minutes. With your consistency, he will soon learn the impetus for the unpleasant shake-can noise, and curb his enthusiasm. He'll simultaneously learn that "legal" chew toys are not only lots of fun, they'll also garner him extra attention from you.

Shake-Can "Recipe"

Take an (empty) soda can and put ten small metal articles in it. Seal with duct tape. To use: When your dog engages in undesirable behavior, shake once. This will startle him and interrupt his behavior. With 100 percent consistency and several repetitions, it can work like a charm. It's important that you give it just a single shake. Any more and he'll desensitize.

Duncan warns that the first several times you correct for chewing, the dog will not associate the "punishment with the crime." Only numerous repetitions, near-perfect consistency, and a saint's patience will accomplish the task and reinforce the desired behavior. Understand that deprogramming the chewing mechanism is an actual remodeling of his inborn nature, so it's unrealistic to expect such radical change in so few exposures.

Following are a few antichewing hints that support Deb Duncan's methods and give credence to the old adage that "an ounce of prevention is worth a pound of cure":

- Chew-proof your house. Pick up all items that could tempt your Westie to chew.
- Keep all socks and shoes out of his reach. If he chews them, it's you who deserves the blame. Do not give him his "own" shoe or sock. It is unrealistic to expect him to distinguish your designer pumps from your old sneakers.
- Carpet edges, couch skirts, and pillows are exceedingly tantalizing to pups' and untrained dogs' mouths. Block their access to these items.
- Don't ever let a pup or untrained dog out of your sight. If he's out of sight and quiet, he's probably contentedly chewing on your trendy new handbag.
- For teething pups, keep nylon bones in your freezer. These are very comforting during teething. A frozen wet rag works well, too.

The secret is to set your Westie up for success. He really does want to please you—even if it means adapting to your rules. And the results will be more than worth your dedicated time and effort.

How Does Your Garden Grow?
Fresh earth, moist earth, mulches, topsoil, and soft dirt or sand are especially enticing to dogs. If you don't barricade off your country garden, you will set the scene for a "digging war." Even if he does not tend to dig—and in Westies, this is pretty much a long shot—your garden will tempt him toward undesirable behavior. If his favorite digging place is in your magnificent flower bed, you may have to securely fence it off to make a lovely cottage garden that your Westie may admire but not decimate.

Digging

Although digging is natural to all dogs, some dogs are more prone to this "industry" than others, and Westies number among this elite group. Other breeds may find alternate impetuses that activate their digging response. Duncan notes that wild dogs dig to bury food, to find food, to hunt quarry, to "make their beds," to create a cool place when it's hot, and to whelp litters. Even a dog who does not dig in the yard will "dig" to adjust his bedding until his place is just right. Then he'll lie down to rest.

"Almost all puppies will have some initial digging behaviors," says Duncan. Sudden onset of digging can result from boredom, an incentive (like a gopher) on the other side of a fence, a neighborhood bitch in season, or grasses starting into growing season—whose roots smell like ambrosia to many dogs. (I am still hopeful that my own terriers will learn to unearth some Oregon white truffles!)

Deterring digging behavior may take a combination of approaches. Duncan recommends

the "shake can" method. Sprays or dry treatments can be sprinkled over an area, but since the deterrent odor is short-lived, the inconvenience of having to refresh the treatment constantly makes it less practical.

When your dog has dug a hole, Duncan suggests, place chicken wire, gravel, or rocks in it and cover it over with dirt. A dog often returns to the same areas he has dug in before, so when he encounters these substances—not exactly his textures of choice—he'll abandon the idea. Putting the dog's feces in the hole and covering it also works with some dogs.

If your dog tries to excavate under your fence, dig a trench around the fence, place chicken wire in it, and cover it. This is a major project but well worth it when you consider the alternative. Stone borders, reinforced cherry-tone logs, and even concrete can keep your Westie from making the great escape. Avoid using any material in a way that could injure your dog.

Try creating an acceptable digging area for your dog. This way, your Westie can dig until the cows come home and you won't have to worry. Select an area and bury toys or treats in it. Demonstrate to him that buried treasures await him underground in this special spot. When you catch him digging where it is verboten, Duncan advises scolding him by saying, "No dig," and replacing him in his designated area. Choose whatever method suits your preference, but remember, no method is a guarantee.

Terriers like Westies are more prone to digging than other breeds.

Did You Know?

Digging is such a major part of terriers' instincts that through adaptation, their nails had to grow faster than most other breeds. If they were left to their own devices, their constant digging would be enough to wear down their nails very quickly—and the nails grow back faster than, say, a sight hound. Therefore, in most domestic environments, Westies need their nails trimmed more frequently than most dogs. Bummer, huh?

Some problem behaviors are a result of lack of attention or boredom.

Growling

A dog's growling sounds are quite diverse, and there are many communication elements and nuances to the sounds he generates. And a Westie's vocal range truly makes him the Julie Andrews of the dog world. But not all growls are negative or aggressive. It's important to assess your dog's growl sounds within a broader context. What (the actual noise) he expresses may differ from how (type of growl) he emits. Certainly there are times when a growl is an unacceptable growl, so becoming a "student of growl-ology" gives you more understanding of your Westie's linguistic capabilities.

Mouthing

Dogs appear to enjoy having mouths. They naturally use their mouths for play and communication. Duncan notes that this is central to their relationships with their mother and littermates. However, in order to harmoniously coexist with humans, puppies must learn new rules. It's our responsibility to show them that we, as caretakers and companions, will not condone mouthing.

You may notice that when your hands are out of reach, your puppy will jump up to try to grab one, hoping to snag it with his puppy teeth. Duncan stresses that this is not aggression: He's really just asking you for interaction and using his mouth to communicate, just as he has seen you use your hands for the same purpose. Again, this presents an opportunity to guide him toward appropriate behavior.

- Any time the puppy's mouth so much as grazes you, "yelp" in pain to startle him.
- With the behavior interrupted, calmly say to him, "No mouth! Good 'no mouth'!"
- Numerous repetitions and several sessions will elapse before he connects your yelp with his own mouth; the key is 100 percent consistency.
- Minimize situations that require you to react.
- Be more careful during playtime; use a toy as a buffer so he will go for that instead of your hand.
- Stay vigilant and decrease opportunities for him grab your hand. You will end up yelping less, and this will help clarify the process for him.

A dog will make mouth contact almost anytime, but during the heightened stimulation and excitement of human/ canine play, the "toy" that he'll go for just happens to be your hand, foot, or ankle. People often mistake this for intentional biting: It's not, insists Duncan. Often, it's just a matter of poor timing and inexact aim. Westies are terriers, and terriers are especially attracted to moving targets.

Noise Phobia

Dogs with noise phobias may react by salivating, hiding, pacing, whining, or panting. Some will even injure themselves in their desperate attempt to escape the stimulus. Hiding in a cool, dark room is a common reaction.

Some phobias will develop gradually; others may surface after a single terrifying experience. Without intervention, a dog may become more afraid with each exposure to the source of his fear. One phobia often leads to others. A dog with a thunder phobia may, by association, become afraid of rain, too. Eventually the rain alone will scare him—even in the absence of thunder. (Then the dog may develop a fear of the state of Oregon.) Whatever the trigger, there is evidence that there is a genetic component to phobias.

The dog that fears thunder and fireworks may be unable to avoid either of them. In mild cases, simply mask the sound by turning on the radio or TV or one of those white noise machines you can get from holistic health outlets. Serious cases may require more radical measures.

Current research suggests that the best approach to curing neutralizing phobias is a two-pronged approach of audio recording desensitization (some kits include strobe lights) and dog-appeasing pheromones (DAPs). Another solution is melatonin, a natural over-the-counter hormone produced by the pineal gland, which can be found in health food stores and also in conventional pharmacies. It has been proven to have a remarkable effect on the "thunderstruck." Some vets will prescribe antianxiety drugs.

Seek help if your dog exhibits possessiveness over certain items or toys.

Possession Aggression: Yours, Mine, or Ours?

Possessiveness is an unacceptable behavior pattern that probably arises from deficient puppy socialization. If your dog stands over his toy or food bowl and stares hard at anyone who deigns to approach him, it is a behavior you need to eliminate immediately. Other signs can include growling, snapping, biting, or not eating.

This type of behavior is actually quite natural. Dogs are programmed to hang on to their sustenance. In the wild, if they give up their bone to another animal, they won't get to eat. However, feral dogs and wolves *will* surrender a meal to the dominant member of the pack. That's you! Ideally, every other human being in your house should precede your dog in the hierarchy. It's doesn't feel natural to every dog, but it's something you must teach him.

With a possessive dog, avoid suddenly snatching his food or toys. This only validates his suspicion that you might be an adversary. Dogs need reassurance that their livelihood is unthreatened. When approaching a dog that seems to be guarding a treat, dog bowl, or toy, try barter. If he's eating kibble, he'll probably trade you for a piece of cheese. (Wouldn't you trade a second-year Ozzie Canseco card for a

Hank Aaron rookie card?) In the case of a more stubborn dog, avoid giving him long-lasting chewing treats altogether—at least until he budges. Give him only small biscuits he can scarf down at once without having to "possess" them.

Teach your Westie to sit and wait before you put his food bowl in front of him. Reward him for his compliance by feeding him a bit of something better than what is in the bowl. (Clue him in, though—or he'll inhale what's in his bowl before you dig the fresh Dungeness crab out of your pocket.)

Keep his food bowl in a large, empty space instead of in a corner. Giving him a "special corner" just reinforces the overprotective behavior you want to eliminate. Move the bowl around; remove it immediately after he's eaten. By staying in the room while he's eating, he'll comprehend that you hold all control over his food.

In established cases of food aggression, take away the dog's food bowl completely and feed him by hand until he realizes that all food comes from you. If he seems suspicious when you approach, drop a tasty piece of food in the bowl every time he eats from your hand.

Always seek professional help with any type of problem behavior that makes you uncomfortable.

Separation Anxiety

One of the most serious psychological problems plaguing the modern domestic dog is separation anxiety. Mostly it's just a dog's flawed attempt to solve what he perceives as a terrible dilemma—being alone, scared, or bored.

Dogs have been selectively bred and conditioned for thousands of years to thrive on human companionship, so when that disappears, some dogs find separation intolerable. They did not evolve to spend hours by themselves. Dogs who have suffered abandonment in the past are especially vulnerable to separation anxiety. They haven't a clue when—or if—you'll return after you leave. For all they know, *this* time could be the "final good-bye."

When they return, owners may find that their freaked-out Westie has taken up some mutant form of interior design. He has "redecorated" the house in grunge style—by adding fringes to your sofa, removing the stuffing from your overstuffed chair, and manifesting other destructive behaviors. He's either cavorting about manically, or he's crouched

Another Dog?

If your dog is alone longer than is good for him, you may wish to get him a companion. Although auxiliary pets are no substitute for people, sometimes having a companion will help. Westie owners who start with one will often later add another.

somewhere in a corner. Once the cycle begins, things tend to worsen because the owner is now drawn into "fearing the unknown." What's next? Aunt Stella's antique rolltop desk with the mother-of-pearl inlay? So the dog picks up the owner's growing tension, and it crescendos as he starts adding more innovative destruction to his repertoire.

Some vets use the generic drug clomimpramine to treat separation anxiety. Though it's no magic bullet and has some undesirable side effects, it's one of several options that might give your anxious Westie some palliative relief, in combination with behavioral measures. (The behavior modification aspect of the therapy is most intensive.) If the owner is committed to working with his dog to conquer the problem, the prognosis for its resolution is good.

To keep both your home and your anxious Westie safe, you may need to confine your dog in your absence. If you'll be gone long, don't crate him. Instead, put him in a large room with a variety of chew toys, a comfortable bed, and access to water. Many dogs with separation anxiety get more agitated when confined, and some will destroy their crates or even self-mutilate in their desperation.

To desensitize your dog to your absences, practice taking "momentary" trips. Practice getting ready to leave (include all your predeparture rituals), but don't actually leave. This helps defuse the energy around the situation by showing him that just because you're going through these activities, it doesn't necessarily mean that it's time for you to go for the day.

When you leave, just go. Don't hang around the house or attempt to placate the dog by cascading him with kisses. He'll just feel worse when you finally withdraw. The more you can ignore him just prior to your departure, the easier the separation will be for him. Provide him with an extra-special toy that he gets only when you leave. Again, treat-stuffed toys work well. Anything that displaces his anxiety will make him feel much better all day. Leave the TV or radio on, but make sure that *Casablanca* isn't playing—the farewell scene between Ingrid Bergman and Humphrey Bogart may be more than he can bear.

Get up a little earlier and take longer walks than usual. Not only will it benefit both of your cardiovascular systems and help produce endorphins, but you may tire him out a tad. A tired dog is a good dog.

Establishing yourself as a trusted leader helps dogs with separation anxiety. As the bond between you strengthens, the dog begins to trust that your decisions are for his own well-being. With that knowledge, your dog can relax.

Separation anxiety doesn't go away on its own, so enlist the help of an experienced behaviorist to deal with this problem.

"True" Aggression

Some truly dangerous aggressive behavior has genetic links, but other causes can include illness or mishandling. If you feel the situation is out of hand, consult a trained behaviorist. Most pet-dog trainers do not have the specialized training needed to deal with aggressive, dangerous dogs, so talk to your veterinarian about finding certified help. A small percentage of dogs are beyond cure, but most are not.

In most cases, owners let aggression happen. Some people allow their dogs to lord over their household. They allow their dog to stake claim to a favorite chair or (in extreme cases) all the furniture. The dog will snatch food, nip children, or defend his food bowls from his owners—who not only put up with it, but also add to the problem.

A well-behaved Westie should do the following:

- Move when told.
- Give up his toys when told.
- Allow any human to approach his food bowl and pet him while he eats. (It's best to allow a dog to eat in peace, but approaching him prepares him for that stray curious child who breaks that rule.)
- Avoid disturbing people while they are eating.
- Avoid nipping unless provoked beyond reason.
- Allow a human to pick him up and carry him.
- Allow his nails to be clipped and his ears cleaned without striking out with his mouth.

Establish early on that you are the boss. In fact, decisiveness is a quality that dogs admire. Your Westie actually wants a good and benevolent leader. To become that leader you must prove yourself worthy with firm, consistent training methods, an even temper, and a no-nonsense attitude. You

Outside activities and exercise are physically and mentally good for your Westie.

get to decide when and where the dog eats, plays, and sleeps.

Some dogs battle for dominion over furniture. To a bossy Westie, furniture can be a fortress, a high place that allows him more status than does the lowly floor. Some dogs equate being elevated with being exalted. So, if he shows any propensities for being bossy, deny him couch privileges until he is ready to surrender them to any human being, including a child, without an altercation. And Westies can certainly be vociferous.

If your dog growls, snarls, or snaps at a person who attempts to "dethrone" him, take firm measures. Strongly prompt him to leave with an unyielding "off!" If he doesn't obey, use a shake can to catch him off guard.

Whenever dealing with an overly assertive dog, stand erect and speak in a firm, no-nonsense voice. Use food to lure your dog off the couch only if he has *not* growled or snapped. A growler will think you're rewarding him for his poor manners. Use the shake can. If you do not achieve success, consult an expert.

HOW TO FIND A CANINE BEHAVIORIST

Never hesitate to seek professional help with your Westie if you need it. Your happiness and his well-being could depend on it. If your dog becomes aggressive toward people or toward other animals or manifests any traits that make you uneasy, immediately seek assistance. Without intervention, it's unlikely that his undesirable behavior will vanish or improve. Your dog needs to learn how to live harmoniously in society. A breed club, your vet, or an obedience instructor may be able to recommend a canine behaviorist. Westie Rescue, both the national group and the regional ones—because they are always wrestling with behavioral issues—maintains contact with competent behaviorists, who've been indispensable to their efforts to safely foster and place Westies with issues.

An animal behaviorist is often an academically trained specialist who's typically completed graduate work in psychology in such specific areas as learning processes, psychoneurology, psychobiology, and zoology. He or she will also have additional experience in dog training and canine behavior.

Among the various behaviors an animal behaviorist treats are phobias, anxiety, aggression (in its many forms and degrees), and obsessive-compulsive disorders. In most cases, a conventional dog trainer lacks the qualifications to treat these cases.

When choosing a canine behaviorist, check out his or her educational credentials; but even more important, ask about the depth of his or her experience and about the kinds of problems he or she has helped solve. The behaviorist should be more than willing to offer you several references from satisfied clients. Behaviorists charge by the hour, but they may also offer treatment programs with set rates based on the individual program. Many will offer phone consultations as well as one-on-one sessions.

Canine behaviorists who also have veterinary degrees sometimes use medications that physicians use on people to treat phobias, aggression, anxiety, and other symptoms. These medications have been proven to be helpful in some cases, but their efficacy is far from perfect. Side effects can, in some instances, add to your problem rather than improve it. The best veterinary canine behaviorists do not use drugs alone, but if they do use them, they combine (and monitor) the medicine with sound behavioral training. Avoid professionals that push a "quick fix" through pill popping.

Canine Aggression 101

- Never provoke a situation where the dog may bite. Chasing him or trying to pull him out of a hiding place is probably a manifestation of a death wish!
- Get your dog vet checked for any possible physical problems. Request a thyroid test.
- Find special training opportunities for aggressive dogs. Regular obedience classes are neither appropriate nor fair to him or to the other dogs and handlers.
- For at least two weeks, restrict your interactions with your dog to a bare minimum; make him beg for your attention.
- Keep the dog completely off the bed, furniture, or other high places.
- Make the dog sit or lie down before feeding him.
- Give your dog twice the exercise he's getting now—outside the yard. Busy dogs have more opportunity to work off stress and are less apt to bite.
- If necessary, keep a soft muzzle on the dog while working with him.
- Keep small children away from the aggressive dog at all times.
- Consult a competent canine behaviorist.
- Avoid any competitive games like tug-of-war. If you do play them, make sure you always win.
- Don't give the dog any toys or possessions at all.

ADVANCED TRAINING AND ACTIVITIES

WITH YOUR WEST HIGHLAND WHITE TERRIER

Your Westie has the basics down and her manners would put Emily Post to shame. But you want more, right? Many fun activities await both of you. However, before leaping into anything, do the following:

- Check out the activity. Do you have the time, money, energy, and interest?
- Assess your Westie's general well-being with a vet before embarking on any new activity.
  - Immerse yourselves gradually, especially in the more intense activities such as agility and flyball.
    - Attend to your Westie's natural limits and take cues from him when he's had enough. Westies are hardy but not invincible.
    - Adjust feeding to sustain your Westie's increased level of activity, if necessary.
    - Stop when either of you has had enough, is tired, injured, or overly frustrated. Never work a sick dog.

COMPETITIVE EVENTS

There are many events you and your Westie can compete in. A number of them are held through the American Kennel Club (AKC). You can find out more about each of these events at www.akc.org or through your local Westie club.

Agility

Agility is an exciting canine sport for both participants and spectators. In this event, a dog demonstrates his athleticism and attentiveness by taking cues from the handler while following a timed obstacle course. The course consists of jumps, tunnels, weave poles, and other obstacles. The activity cements bonds between dog and handler and provides fun and vigorous exercise for both.

AKC Agility, which debuted in the United States in 1994, is currently the fastest-growing dog sport in the country. All AKC-approved breeds are eligible for this canine sport. A standard agility course contains 20 obstacles spread over about 180 yards (171.9 m). Most competitive dogs cover this distance in 50 seconds or less. To level the playing field, different jump heights accommodate each breed of dog either according to the dog's actual height or his physical limitations.

Agility consists of obstacles like weave poles, dog walks, and jumps.

The height your Westie will be required to jump is determined by measuring his height at the withers, which may not exceed the height of the jump itself. Most Westies jump somewhere around 12 inches (30 cm), give or take 2 inches (5 cm). Adjustments in the expected time to complete the course also accommodate the less athletic breeds.

AKC Agility offers two types of classes. The Standard Class includes multiple obstacles such as the dog walk, the A-frame, and seesaw. The Jumpers with Weaves classes contain only jumps and weave poles. Both classes offer opportunities to earn novice, open, excellent, and master titles. After completing both excellent standard and excellent jumpers titles, a dog-handler team can compete for the "supersonic" Master Agility Champion (MACH) title. The dogs run the same course, with adjustments in the expected time. To equalize competition between the different sizes of dogs, classes are divided by jump heights.

Westies continue to add to the elite ranks of agility. More than 48 have attained the excellence level of the sport.

Canine Good Citizen Test

In 1989, the AKC initiated the Canine Good Citizen (CGC) program to reward dogs and their owners who've socialized their dogs to behave well at home and in their communities. This two-part program promotes responsible pet ownership.

Any dog—purebred or mixed—who passes the ten-step test is eligible for official certification from the American Kennel Club. In addition to nurturing the dog/owner relationship, CGC training is excellent preparation for formal obedience work. Obedient dogs are not only wonderful companions, they also adjust well to household routines and demonstrate good etiquette toward people and other dogs—enough to impress Miss Manners. Your Westie will be grateful that you considered him important enough to invest the time to train, stimulate, and care for him, and you will have a certificate to prove it.

Earthdog Tests

AKC Earthdog tests provide opportunities to measure your dog's instinctual hunting and working abilities, and many Westies have excelled at this. AKC currently offers four

This Westie has entered in the tunnel in an earthdog competition.

levels: a "nontitling" class, Introduction to Quarry (a basic exposure to earthwork), Junior Earthdog (JE), Senior Earthdog (SE), and Master Earthdog (ME). The first two are essentially instinct tests, the last two are ostensibly designed to replicate actual hunting situations.

All tests include a den with tunnels and turns, which become progressively more complex at each ascending level. Each 9-inch (22.9 cm) diameter wood-lined tunnel ends with a cage of (often terminally bored) rats. The judge sprays the path to the quarry with "rat tea," a delightful concoction derived from urine-soaked rat-cage shavings.

Flyball

Though not an official AKC event, flyball is a team sport for dogs that started in California almost 30 years ago. Its first appearance on the popular *Johnny Carson Show* offered widespread exposure. Soon it captured the fancy of dog trainers and dog clubs everywhere. In the early 1980s, due to flyball's infectious popularity, the North American Flyball Association (NAFA) formed.

With four dogs on each team, flyball is a relay race. The 51-foot-long (15.5 m) course consists of a starting line, 4 hurdles spaced 10 feet (3 m) apart, and a spring-loaded box that ejects a tennis ball. Each dog jumps the hurdles and steps on the box. After catching the ejected ball, he clears the hurdles to cross the starting line, prompting the next dog to go. The first team to have all four dogs run without errors wins the heat.

Did You Know?

Many other countries (including England, Australia, Japan, Hungary, Denmark, Sweden, Canada, and Finland) have developed programs based on the AKC's CGC program. A CGC Neighborhood Model has been established; police and animal control agencies use CGC for dealing with dog problems in communities; some therapy-dog groups use CGC as a partial-screening tool; and some 4-H groups have been using CGC as a beginning dog-training program for children.

Flyball is a fast-paced relay race where dogs catch tennis balls and race over hurdles.

Tournaments are either a double elimination or round robin. In both cases, each member of the first team to win three heats out of five receives 1 point towards his standing.

The shortest dog's stature determines the hurdle heights—4 inches (10 cm) below the shoulder height of the shortest dog for an 8-inch (20 cm) minimum height and a 16-inch (40.6 cm) maximum. Shorter dogs, such as speedy, ball-crazy Westies are coveted by teams of Border Collies, for instance, since lower hurdles can shave seconds off the team's total time. The faster the times, under a maximum of 32 seconds, the more points each dog on the team receives.

Obedience

Obedience trials test a dog's ability to work with his handler and perform prescribed scored exercises. These trials emphasize the usefulness of the purebred dog as an animal companion. Novice, or first-level AKC competitive obedience exercises, include heeling on lead, standing for examination, coming when called, heeling off lead, and remaining in both a sit and a down position until the handler is instructed by the judge to release the dog. For the levels after novice (open and utility) the exercises get increasingly complicated.

Although Westies are not considered a "conventional" obedience breed, they are nevertheless trainable and can make quite an impression in the obedience ring. The feisty attitude and keen intelligence typical of Westies can result in very good obedience competitors. Though originally selectively bred for their independent problem-solving abilities, Westies are loyal to their humans, and the opportunity to work together can result—and has resulted—in top-notch obedience dogs.

Rally Obedience

Rally officially became an AKC titling event in 2005. According to Westie owner and performance enthusiast Roz Rosenblatt, rally is like obedience—only laid-back. Unlike conventional obedience, your dog doesn't have to work at perfect heel position. You are encouraged to praise and communicate with your dog. Precision, attitude, and enthusiasm rate high in this event. In rally, you and your Westie work as real partners.

Numbered signs that provide specific instructions mark each of 10 to 20 stations on a rally course. The number of

A Westie completing a station at a rally course.

signs and the complexity of the instructions increase at each level. At the novice level, as in the corresponding level in conventional AKC Obedience, dogs work on lead, and exercises are basic. As dog-handler duo progresses, the sport becomes more challenging and includes some jumping and work off lead. Speed is not critical and is only used as a tiebreaker. With a score of 70 percent out of a possible 100 percent, you and your dog qualify for one of three legs required for a title.

You can practice at home: All you need are the cones and rally signs and—later—an 8-inch (20 cm) jump, which you can order from AKC. Rosenblatt finds this time relaxing and rewarding for herself and her Westies. Not bad for a competitive event!

Showing (Conformation)

Dog shows (conformation events) are intended to evaluate breeding stock. Therefore, only sexually intact dogs qualify for conventional AKC conformation events. The size of these events ranges from large all-breed shows, with entries of over 3,000 dogs, to small local specialty-club shows featuring a specific breed. The dog's overall appearance and

Showing Tip

Caution: Excessive repetition may result in boredom or "creative improvisation" in the show ring. But if you keep things interesting and challenging, your Westie should rise to the occasion.

structure, or conformation—often an indication of the dog's ability to produce quality puppies—is judged. There are three types of conformation dog shows, as follows:

- All-breed shows offer competitions for over 150 breeds and varieties of dogs recognized by the AKC. All-breed shows are the type often shown on television.
- Specialty shows are restricted to dogs of a specific breed or to varieties of one breed.
- Group shows are limited to dogs belonging to one of the seven AKC groups.

Conformation shows are where you expect to see Westies that look like Westies and Shar-Peis that look unmistakably Shar-Pei-ish. Numerous opportunities to show your Westie to his championship title abound. Like flea markets and horse shows, you can find one nearly every weekend of the year—holidays included. The AKC alone hosts 15,000 various competition events. While there can be only one Best in Show, there are lots of ribbons go around at each show.

If your dog is show quality, your responsible hobby breeder or knowledgeable members of a local Westie club will honestly help you assess his chances of attaining his Championship. Showing a dog, however, is hardly as easy as it appears. That's the paradox: It requires a lot of skill to make it look easy. Training your dog to "stack" (pose properly), to stand still while being examined, and to "show his heart out" requires practice. It takes more than good conformation and flashy movement to make a winner. It's that hypnotic *je ne sais quoi* that tells the judge, "You will pick me!" Many gorgeous dogs simply lack the necessary attitude to achieve the top levels or even finish a championship. A beautiful dog with the personality of tapioca pudding is unlikely to win shows.

For most people, that top level is an AKC Championship. It takes 15 points, including 2 majors (wins of 3, 4 or 5 points) awarded by at least 3 different judges, to become an American Kennel Club "Champion of Record." Judges examine the dogs, then give awards according to how closely each dog compares to their mental image of the "perfect" dog as described in the breed's official standard.

A dog show is really an elimination contest. Male dogs compete against males (called "dogs") and females against females (called "bitches"—their proper appellation) in each

Breed Standard & Type

The breed standard describes the characteristics that allow the breed to perform the function for which it was bred. These standards include specifications for structure, temperament, and movement.

Breed type clearly distinguishes one breed from another. My own definition of type includes the word quintessence—as in Westie-ness. A so-called typey dog's physical appearance and bearing fairly yells out the breed standard.

breed, with the best of each sex being awarded points toward his or her championship.

Do It Yourself or Bring in the Pros?

Many Westie breeders and owners enjoy showing their dogs themselves. For various reasons, other owners cannot show or don't enjoy it, and they hire a professional handler.

So what do you look for in a professional handler? Breeder and handler Linda Wells stresses that a handler should be honest with you. If she does not believe that your dog is of show quality, she should tell you so—even at the risk of losing a potential client. This is a hallmark of a responsible handler.

Another successful professional terrier handler, Sally George, elaborates, "Watch your potential handler at shows before you consider contracting her services." Do the handler's "charges" appear happy and in good physical condi-

Westies competing in the show ring.

Westminster and Crufts

The most famous dog show in the United States is Westminster, where only AKC Champions are eligible to compete. It used to be a mad race to get entries in. As a result, many top-ranked dogs did not make the entry. Now the five top-ranked dogs of each breed receive an invitation which, if accepted, guarantees entry.

The United Kingdom has Crufts, a somewhat more informal show than Westminster. Run by the Kennel Club, it features 197 different breeds (more than the 150 currently recognized in the United States). The original Cruft, named Charles, made his living selling dog cakes all across Europe. Inspired by the multiplicity of breeds, he organized the first show in 1891. Today in the United Kingdom, there are basically two kinds of shows: open shows, which are informal, even casual, and champion shows, which are much more competitive.

tion? How does he or she interact with the dogs? George brings up several additional important questions and criteria, as follows:

- How does the handler care for her dogs? Does she have the facility, equipment, ability, and experience to properly care for yours?
- Does the handler have the skill to groom and condition a Westie so that it will be competitive? Look for other Westies he's shown. Get some show pictures of the handler's top-winning dogs. At a glance, do the dogs he handles look like winners?
- Do the handler's dogs make a good first impression? George stresses that Westies are a highly-trimmed breed, so the show-ring judging—for better or for worse—is generally based 50 percent on dog and 50 percent on presentation. Judges have only two and a half minutes to totally evaluate each dog, so first impressions are crucial.

Seek a handler with whom you can communicate. You need to understand why the handler will not show your dog on a particular weekend and where he or she wants to take her. Communication fosters trust, which is essential to any relationship.

You're entrusting your precious Westie to this person. It's imperative that you feel assured that your dog will receive the best treatment possible. Do not tolerate any handler that lies to you or mistreats your dog. Once your trust is violated, find another handler.

What to Wear

Breeder Sandy Davis follows the following sensible rules when exhibiting her Westies:

- Dress to complement the color of the dog and to subtly enhance his appearance. This means that you dress conservatively: no jeans, shorts, miniskirts, or low necklines—and nothing too tight.
- Blue, gray, black, red, green, and even purple complement a white dog. Brown, tan, and yellow do not, as they tend to shed their color onto the dog. Turquoise works well with any breed or color of dog. Plaids or prints, unless very muted, are too busy and detract from the dog. Neat casual clothing is all right at the class level.
- If you are "specialing" a dog, or competing at the group level or beyond, consider something more formal like a suit or pantsuit.
- Wear sensible shoes with low heels in neutral browns, tans, grays, or black. Rubber-cushioned soles work well for comfort and function.

Tracking

Are you seeking a pleasurable outdoor activity for your Westie? Why not tracking? Consider this: A German Shepherd has 220 million olfactory cells, compared to a human's measly 5 million. This number varies according to breed: Longer-muzzled dogs have an advantage over brachiocephalic (flat-faced) dogs. Though relatively short muzzled, your Westie has a bumper crop of these cells and proves it as you watch him track naturally, identifying scents of various animals and people who have passed his way on your

How to Earn an English Championship

In the United Kingdom, a dog must win Best Bitch or Best Dog at a championship show three times to earn Championship Certificates (or CCs). The dogs first compete in classes according to age or place of origin. In UK competitions, four-month-old puppies may compete, whereas in the United States, entrants must be at least six months of age. The judge selects the winner from among the winners of each class (again divided by gender). There is no age limit, but if a puppy gets three CCs before he turns a year old (and this is highly unlikely), he has to wait until after he's turned a year old to become a champion.

In the United Kingdom, exhibitors usually wait until a dog is fully mature before showing him in earnest. In contrast, in the States, many dogs have attained their championships before their first birthday.

This Westie, "Sprite," has the distinction of being the only Champion Tracker terrier to date.

walks. He'll try to follow the interesting ones—even if you have other ideas. So to succeed in competitive tracking, you must surrender to his prowess because he, not you, is the expert. Through tracking, the two of you will forge the closest of bonds, and your respect for your Westie's ability will grow along with your relationship.

In competition, a judge will choose the scent for your Westie to follow. A properly trained dog can follow a path someone has taken five hours earlier. He will successfully find and carry an article—often a glove—imbued with that person's scent.

Individuals differ in aptitude, but AKC Tracking Judge Allison Platt suggests that tracking may be an appropriate "prelude" to formal obedience or agility training. A younger dog not yet taught to totally rely on you for guidance may have an advantage. He often has no qualms about pulling you—this is actually desirable in tracking—and loves working so much that he couldn't care less whether you're behind him or not. Older, more self-reliant dogs may also do well. But for any Westie, tracking is a great confidence builder; it also gives the two of you an opportunity to embark on adventures both rewarding and healthful.

A minimum of equipment, as follows, will get you started tracking:

- a nonrestrictive harness for your Westie, and a 40-foot line
- some personal articles with your scent on them (gloves or socks, for instance)
- surveyors' flags or brightly spray-painted clothespins to mark your training tracks
- weather-resistant clothes—just the rationalization you need for buying more clothing!

The Nose Knows

What if your nose were as sensitive as your Westie's? With his nose, he "sees" a whole network of paths as acutely as if they were strewn with distinct multicolored lines. Tracking theory suggests that a dog can glom onto one of these scent paths and follow it to its conclusions, as easily as a person can connect the dots to form a picture.

Versatility

The West Highland White Terrier Club of America's Versatile Dog program was the brainchild of William (Sil) Sanders. The Versatile Dog Award program awards Westies who achieve certain high levels of accomplishment in their lifetimes. Awards are based on a point system in which each level of achievement in an area earns a point. The areas Westies compete in are conformation, obedience, tracking, agility, and earthdog.

In 1980, Ch. Skaket's Chunkies, UD, CG became the first Versatile Dog. The program flourished to become one of the most impressive AKC Versatility programs in the United States.

A Versatile Dog has won points by competing in events like agility and obedience.

NONCOMPETITIVE ACTIVITIES

You may decide that organized events just aren't for you and your Westie. Never fear—there are plenty of exercises and games you can play together at home that will keep your dog's mind and body occupied, and increase the bond between the two of you.

Fun and Games

The following are some favorite games Westie owners play with their dogs:

- Nancy's Westie Andy loves playing with a giant kick ball. He likes when it is thrown, so he can chase it and try to bite it.
- Westie Sophie enjoys being chased around the house in order to capture her favorite toy. The exercise benefits both Sophie and her owner, Vicki. But her absolute favorite thing is to bat and chase empty plastic milk jugs.

Non-Westie Events

AKC rules do not permit Westies to compete in lure coursing, herding, or hunting trials, although I recently met a Westie with the most perfect point! Come to think about it, it's not that they would be unable to do some of these events. Many fun days with terriers include an informal kind of lure coursing—they certainly don't lack the prey drive. Herding is a little trickier. Some Westies might do quite well at it, and I have heard of terriers imbued with this instinct, but others might see the ducks more as an all-you-can-eat buffet rather than as something to herd and care for.

While Westies don't officially participate in hunting trials, some still know how to point.

- Evy's Westie, Thurston, likes to catch her. It's a game of mutual keep-away. Also, like many other Westies, he loves to compete with 65-pound dog (and housemate) Archie, and knock the tennis ball thrown for Archie out of the dog's mouth.
- Riley inherited a collection of stuffed ladybugs, which he enjoys chasing when Karen goads him on. Another tennis ball chaser, he soon learned that linoleum can be slippery, so he works fast to intercept it before the carpet ends and the bare floor begins.
- Charlie is a soccer goalie. When owner Wilma tosses the tennis ball, he blocks it. She also hides and challenges him to find her just by calling his name. Tracking with kibble or cereal is another favorite.
- Nancy's Westie, Fergus, herds his blue basketball all over the house and yard while barking with great enthusiasm.
- Hampton is another compulsive ball retriever. Peggy says he enjoys barking at squirrels, as do many Westies. He and Westie sibling Abby play tug-o-war with Hampton's chew bunny.
- Joan and her Westie push a ball back and forth between them and play catch. They conclude with a high five, and for his finale he rolls over and "chills out."
- Matt's Westie, Brodie, loves empty 2-liter soda bottles, proving that the best toys are often the cheapest. Brodie picks one up by the cap and watches it roll and make strange noises. He tries to stalk it (carefully, of course, so as not to alert it). However, his favorite tug toy is an inch-wide 6-foot nylon leash. By cutting off the buckle,

Matt allowed the end to fray, and Brodie is entertained for hours while Matt grips the loop grip. The bonus is that it helped him learn to walk much better on leash because he no longer chews his real leash—he knows that playtime is coming with the "fake" one. Brodie also enjoys finding hidden toys.

- Dawn Martin reports, "My dogs enjoy a good game of 'bobbing for hotdogs.'" She uses a big basin of water, and her dogs literally go to great depths for each morsel. This well-known breeder of conformation and performance star Westies adds that this game trains them to use their noses.

- Kathy's Westie Nicky plays "whatever game he chooses." He trolls Kathy and her husband for kisses. He also has a penchant (checked) for shredding toilet paper, so Kathy removes that temptation from the roller in her bathroom.

(Thanks to the Westie aficionados at Westie-l, an e-mail list dedicated to all things Westie, for sharing their fun and games.)

Walking and Jogging

Walking or jogging with your Westie will benefit both of you. Remember that your Westie is a terrier, vulnerable to the lure of the occasional errant squirrel as it scurries across the street. That, in addition to leash laws, should compel you to keep him on a leash at all times. Westie endurance is amazing. Barring disability or old age, Westies are little canine bundles of energy. Just be sure to check with your vet before starting any strenuous activity with your dog.

Robust, hardy terriers that they are, Westies are often eager, able, and willing to walk for miles without showing signs of fatigue—even if you do! Be sure to bring along some extra water for him *and* yourself. However, in hot weather, take it easy—consider abbreviating your outing to avoid dangerous heatstroke.

THERAPY WORK

Therapy dogs comfort the sick, cheer the elderly, and enhance the lives of those with whom their paths cross. That they provide benefits for heart patients, AIDS patients, people with disabilities, children with autism, and people with

Gossip and Sportsmanship

If you criticize a dog while he's in the ring, your rudeness is guaranteed to bite you in the back. You will unwittingly be standing at ringside beside the owner or breeder of the dog you just demeaned. Lack of cooperation, respect, and communication can only harm all involved, robbing the event of the potential for fellowship forged by a common goal of showing and breeding the best dogs possible.

other disorders has been well documented. They also can visit nursing homes, homeless shelters, and hospitals. Therapy dogs have even played key roles in the rehabilitation of convicted criminals in prisons.

It's best to have your Westie certified—either by the facility you'll be visiting or by a pet-assisted therapy organization. Even a Canine Good Citizen certificate will suffice for some facilities. At a basic level, you'll be making rounds, interacting with patients or residents, and providing a great service, since many of these people get limited opportunity for meaningful interaction of any kind. At more complex levels, you and your dog may participate in prescribed therapy plans.

Certification programs vary, but most require a certain level of obedience and a health screening. Most also require that the dog be at least a year old. He should be clean and free of fleas. Friendliness, obedience, and good communication between you and your Westie are essential. To find out what programs are available in your area, contact a local nursing home or hospital. Two national organizations, Therapy Dogs International (TDI) and the Delta Society offer nationwide accreditation programs. Other organizations offer certification as well.

A well-behaved Westie can make a terrific therapy dog—and a bit of a novelty too, since larger dogs make up the majority of those doing this type of work. The portable, stable Westie may gladly play the role of "love sponge" on a patient's lap, lie on someone's bed, perform a few selections from a repertoire of remarkable tricks, or dispense kisses—

if that's what's wanted and needed. Westies have provided solace to hospitalized people of all ages, listened—without judgment—to stories read by children with learning disabilities, and brightened many days at nursing homes.

If you don't want to participate in organized sports, there's still plenty of fun to be had with your Westie.

HEALTH

OF YOUR WEST HIGHLAND WHITE TERRIER

In general, among purebred dogs, Westies are considered a hardy and sturdy breed. Remember that no dog—purebred or mixed breed—is immune to health problems. Environmental as well as genetic predispositions can factor into any dog's well-being. Since you want your Westie to live a long, joyful, and comfortable life, proper home care and plenty of TLC are important. Also essential for his optimum health is regular veterinary care—both for preventative and prompt and competent treatment for any problems that arise. If you are concerned about any aspect of your Westie's well-being, it's always better to seek veterinary advice than to worry yourself to shreds. Err on the side of caution.

FINDING A VETERINARIAN

After you, your veterinarian is your dog's best friend. To find the right vet, ask people who share your own approach to pet care. Seek recommendations from your Westie's breeder, friends, dog trainers, or your pet sitter. Telephone directories provide important information about hours, services, and staff. And don't wait until you really need one to find a vet—start looking as soon as you know you are getting a dog.

When looking for a veterinarian, make sure to check out the facility, and request a tour. You're looking for someone to meet both your needs and your Westie's—a doctor who has people skills as well "crate-side manners." Try to assess the entire veterinary team's competence and their people skills. If you like the veterinarian but dislike the staff, keep looking. If the fees are a bargain yet you're uncomfortable about some other aspect of the facility, move on. The longer drive or slightly higher fees could pay "healthy" dividends.

Membership in the American Animal Hospital Association (AAHA) signifies that a veterinary hospital has voluntarily pursued and met prescribed standards in most important areas of animal care. Board certification in veterinary specialties such as ophthalmology, surgery, or cardiology indicates that a vet studied for an additional two to four years in the specialty and passed a rigorous examination.

After narrowing your search, schedule a visit to meet the staff, and discuss the hospital's philosophy and policies. Following are some questions to ask and points to observe:
- Are appointments required?
- How many veterinarians are in the practice?
- Are there technicians or other professional staff members?

- Is the facility clean, comfortable, and well organized?
- Is the staff caring, calm, competent, and courteous, and do they communicate effectively?
- Do the veterinarians have special interests such as geriatrics or behavior?
- Do the fees fit your budget, and are discounts for senior citizens or multipet households available?
- Are X-rays, ultrasound, blood work, EKG, endoscopies, and other diagnostics done in-house or referred to a specialist?
- What emergency services are available?
- Is the vet familiar with Westies and their special needs?
- What services does the clinic provide? Boarding? Grooming? Home visits?
- Are any of the staff specialists?
- What hours is the clinic open? Is there a vet on call during off-hours?
- How close is the vet to your home? (I have discovered that having more than one vet can work well. One is close to home, and another, though farther away, I'll visit for particular issues.)
- Does the clinic accept pet insurance?

PARTNERS IN HEATH

As our animals' guardians, caregivers, and advocates, we must educate ourselves. If we don't take the responsibility and make informed choices regarding our pets' well-being, no one else will. Learn to recognize the first signs of illness, and see your veterinarian regularly for preventive visits. If your pet is not well, don't wait until he is really sick before calling your veterinarian. Remember that Westies are notorious for their stoicism, so your dog may not appear as ill as he really is.

We're the ones who make the ultimate decisions regarding our pets. The vet's extra training and medical knowledge merit respect, but that does not preclude our own research and our responsibility for asking the right questions. A caring veterinarian shares our concern for our dog's well-being. Ideally, it's a partnership, and you and the vet should share some similar philosophies and hold each other in mutual respect. If you feel your needs as a client or those of your pet are unsatisfactorily met, find a new veterinarian. This applies to both allopathic and holistic, or alternative, vets.

If your dog has been diagnosed with a serious ailment, do ask the following tough questions:

- "What is wrong with my Westie?" Get both the official medical name for the disorder and a layperson's explanation of its meaning.
- "What's his prognosis?" Is the disease curable? Manageable? If not, is it fatal?
- "What's the best course of action?" Your vet may want to do surgery, radiation, herbal therapy, or acupuncture, so you need to find out what he or she wants to do and its potential benefits. (I often ask my vet, "If he were your dog, what would you do?")
- "How will this disease and its treatment affect my dog?" Will he lose his appetite, become incontinent, and so on? Is the disease contagious?
- "What's my role?" You may need to medicate him regularly or take him to a special clinic.

- "How much will this cost?" This important query can prevent disputes.
- "Should my Westie see a specialist?" Asking your general practitioner vet for a recommendation for a specialist is neither inappropriate nor insulting. Your vet may get to this question before you do.

Get everything in writing, and stay until you understand completely. If you later realize you forgot to ask something, call back for clarification. If you are dissatisfied with anything about your Westie's treatment, consider switching vets. Furthermore, it is perfectly OK to seek a second opinion or an alternative treatment.

You also want to make sure you do your part to make your veterinarian's job easier. Schedule appointments, be

You and your veterinarian should work together for your Westie's health.

punctual, and for everyone's safety, bring your dog to the clinic on a leash or in a carrier. If you have an emergency, call ahead to ensure that the veterinarian is available. If not, request a referral to an emergency clinic. Post your veterinarian's office number near your telephone. Unless you have a special arrangement with her, do not disturb your veterinarian during nonworking hours for nonemergencies.

PUPPY'S FIRST VISIT

The exam actually begins before the vet even touches your dog. You'll fill out forms, answer questions, and provide information. Everything you know about your puppy and convey to the vet can ensure your dog's wellness.

The exam usually starts with a weigh-in and a check of the nose and mouth, which includes a dental exam. For puppies, the vet will look at the deciduous teeth, and then examine the face and head to check the neurological function of the cranial nerves. Then the vet will examine the ears.

A check for fleas and signs of allergy and infection will follow. The vet will palpate the neck to rule out abnormalities in the lymph nodes or thyroid area.

The vet will also palpate the dog's muscles and extend and bend the dog's legs to test for reflexes or pain on motion. Let your vet check the puppy's patellas; do not manipulate them yourself as this may actually cause damage—this is a specific skill. The exam proceeds with a listen to the dog's heart and lungs through a stethoscope and an external exam of the kidneys, liver, and intestines. An experienced examiner can spot abnormalities by touch or by a painful reaction from the puppy. The vet will take your puppy's temperature and perform a simple rectal exam.

If your Westie puppy is due for immunizations, your vet will make sure that he is following the prescribed schedule and administer them as needed.

SPAYING AND NEUTERING

If you're not planning on entering the wild, wooly world of exhibiting and breeding your Westie, seriously consider spaying or neutering your dog. This not only cuts down on the unwanted dog population, but it can have health benefits as well.

When you spay your bitch, you're removing the entire reproductive system, thus eliminating any possibility of future uterine infections and cancers, and ovarian tumors. Spaying before her first heat cycle (six months is a good time) essentially ensures that she will never develop mammary tumors. There is still a probability reduction if you spay after one or two estrus cycles, but after three of four, that benefit ends. However, she will not attract unwanted suitors once she is spayed.

Neutering your male early has advantages as well. Male-to-male aggression rarely develops into an issue with neutered dogs. Furthermore, neutering eliminates the wanderlust asso-

Good to Know

Unless you're a responsible breeder, you'll want to avoid having intact Westies of opposite sexes under one roof. Otherwise, about twice a year, your life will be a living hell. Your Westie girl will turn into a strumpet, and your Westie boy will turn into an alien version of an oversexed teenage boy.

ciated with his finding his "dream bitch." (Canine standards are generally low.) The risks associated with prostate and testicular cancers disappear. This benefit remains even if the procedure is done later in life. In older males, indoor marking either vanishes or reduces significantly. Generally, the earlier you neuter, the better the chance that the behavior will disappear, but this varies with each individual.

Spaying and neutering can have health benefits for your dog.

Advances in anesthesia, and veterinarians who routinely perform these sterilizations minimize the risks. Recovery is speedy, but keeping your Westie from overdoing it the day after surgery may take diligence. Given the Westie's determination, enforced crate rest works best.

Before surgery, follow your vet's pre-op instructions. And make sure you follow any instructions for a speedy recovery—some vets will require you to return, to remove stitches. Others use self-dissolving sutures.

VACCINATIONS

The purpose of a vaccine is to prompt an animal's immune response against a specific disease. The vaccine stimulates the immune system with a virus or bacteria that has been killed or modified in such a way that it no longer poses a danger to the pet. The dog then develops "memory cells" that help it fight off the dangerous disease-causing form of the virus he is exposed to it.

In order to obtain the best response, puppies and unvaccinated older dogs receive repeated doses. The first shot primes the immune system, and subsequent inoculations boost the immune response. Usually the second vaccine is given two to four weeks after the first. If too long a period elapses, the immune system loses its "jump start" and will not produce a sufficient immune response. (This doesn't apply to rabies vaccines, however.)

Newborn puppies receive some protection (antibodies) from their mothers' bodies and then from their milk. Only when the maternal antibodies drop, after weaning, will a commercial vaccine be effective. However, there is a period when the maternal antibodies are too low to protect but still high enough to block the vaccine. Unfortunately, this period coincides with the time when the puppy is most at risk for many viral diseases. The length and timing of this window is variable among different litters and even among different puppies.

Below is a sample puppy vaccination schedule. It is not an endorsement of any particular regime.

Vaccination Protocols

Proper vaccinations can save lives. Before the days of effective veterinary vaccines, dogs often succumbed to canine distemper, hepatitis, and rabies. Now these diseases are rare. When parvo first emerged in the late 1970s, countless dogs died until a vaccine was developed. However, vaccination protocols have changed over the years, and it's important to discuss this issue with your veterinarian. There is ongoing discussion about how often and against what illnesses dogs need to be vaccinated. Consult with your veterinarian to ask about his or her vaccine protocol. Opinions on commercial vaccinations, schedules, and even on whether to vaccinate at all vary greatly and are subjects of much debate.

The most recent research supports a new protocol for vaccinating your Westie, recommending minimal vaccine use. On recommendations from Dr. Jean Dodds, one of the leading authorities on canine immune systems, all 27 veterinary schools in North America are in the process of changing their protocols for vaccinating dogs and cats.

Did You Know?

According to the American Veterinary Medical Association, dogs at low risk of disease exposure may not need annual boosters for most diseases. Consult with your veterinarian to determine the appropriate vaccination schedule for your dog.

Diseases to Vaccinate Against

Following are the diseases a Westie will most commonly be vaccinated against:

Bordetella

Bordetellosis, or "kennel cough," is like a bad cold in older dogs but can be serious in puppies. Many organisms can cause this condition, which is highly contagious. Infected dogs cough, wheeze, and sneeze. The common vaccine does not protect against all its forms because there are so many. The disease is often self-limiting, but can threaten a dog whose health is otherwise compromised.

Coronavirus

Coronavirus is related to the human cold. Vaccination is recommended solely in areas where the illness is rampant. Most serious in puppies, corona passes through food contaminated by an infected dog's feces. This virus produces symptoms similar to those of parvovirus, but less severe. There is no real cure for this disease, only management.

Distemper

Distemper destroys the nervous system, attacking every tissue in the body. Caused by an airborne, measles-like virus, incubation period is 7 to 21 days. Initial symptoms of lethargy, fever, runny nose, yellow discharge from the eyes, labored breathing, and appetite loss progress to a nervous twitch and thickening of the pads and nose. By this stage, recovery is unlikely.

Hepatitis

Hepatitis, caused by an adenovirus, is most dangerous in puppies. Contact with an infected dog or with his urine or feces spreads hepatitis, causing white-blood-cell-count drops and sometimes clotting problems. It also affects the kidneys and liver. Symptoms include high fever, red mucus membranes, depression, and appetite loss. Even dogs who recover can experience subsequent chronic illnesses; they may also shed the virus for months, which makes this highly contagious. Due largely to the effectiveness of the vaccination, this disease is rare nowadays.

Rabies

Regarding vaccinations, rabies is a special case since it is so deadly and is transmittable to people. You must vaccinate your dog according to local regulations.

Leptospirosis

The bacterially caused leptospirosis can transmit to human beings. Dogs contract this disease through exposure to the urine of infected animals. Affecting the liver and kidney, in its most dangerous form it can cause renal failure. Even if the dog survives the disease, he can sustain permanent kidney damage. Treatment includes antibiotics and, in severe cases, dialysis. A vaccine is available for some forms of lepto, but many vets do not recommend it, especially for young puppies. The "older" strains of lepto are rare, and the vaccine can cause adverse reactions in some dogs. A new, virulent strain, one previously seen only in horses and cows, is on the rise. A vaccine against this form is being tested.

Lyme Disease

Lyme disease, carried by the deer tick and first identified in the 1970s in Old Lyme, Connecticut, has spread to other parts of the country but is prevalent in the Northeast. Incubation period is from 2 to 5 months. It causes acute, intermittent lameness, fever, and heart and kidney disease. If untreated, your dog can develop arthritis. Consider this vaccine if your dog lives in a risky area and spends a lot of time in wooded areas.

Parvo

The virulent, deadly parvovirus first appeared in 1978. Transmitted through the feces of infected dogs, it invades and destroys fast-growing cells in multiple vital organs. Nausea, depression, vomiting, and severe bloody diarrhea result. The disease can be mild to fatal; puppies are especially vulnerable. Unfortunately, parvo is cold resistant, surviving in infected feces at temperatures as low as 20°F (-6°C). Incubation period is from two to seven days.

Rabies

Rabies is a deadly neurological viral disease transmitted through the bite of an infected animal. Rabies vaccinations remain mandatory everywhere in the United States. Immunize puppies against this disease by six months of age.

DISEASES THAT MAY AFFECT YOUR WESTIE

The following are some problems that may affect Westies.

The breed is fairly sound with fewer problems than many other breeds, but every breed is susceptible to specific problems while practically "immune" to others. It's useful to be aware of these diseases' existence, but there is no need to anticipate any of them.

Addison's Disease

Addison's disease is characterized by a complete loss of function of both adrenal glands, which help maintain the normal levels of sodium, potassium, and glucose in the dog's blood. Most cases result from an autoimmune process—the dog's immune system attacks its own adrenal glands.

Addison's disease is most common among young to middle-aged dogs and more common in females. Typical symptoms are lethargy, lack of appetite, vomiting, and weight loss—often severe. Other symptoms can include a slower-than-normal heart rate, and dehydration. The clinical signs are vague and in no way conclusively diagnostic of Addison's disease.

Abnormally high blood potassium levels and lower-than-normal blood sodium levels are key indicators. Blood count

Proper vaccination can save your Westie's life.

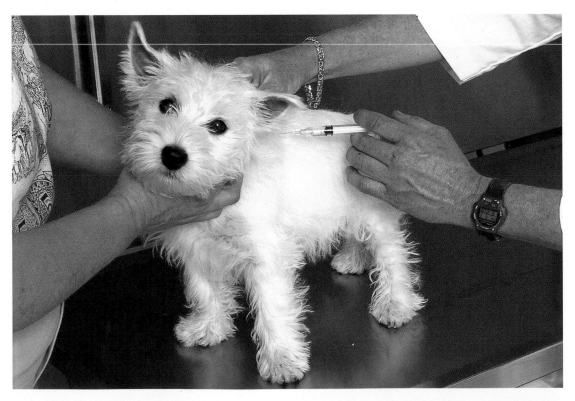

and chemistry profile determinations help with the diagnosis. Replacement steroid therapy comprises Addison's main treatment. With the appropriate treatment, stress reduction, and follow-up care, the prognosis is good, and the affected dog should have a normal life expectancy.

Atopic Dermatitis

Atopic dermatitis (AD) is a common skin condition in dogs typically caused by airborne allergens such as dander, pollens of grasses, weeds, or trees, and house dust or molds. Some Westies seem to be able to tolerate these; others do not.

The airborne allergens are inhaled, make initial contact with the upper respiratory system, then enter the body and interact with cells—resulting in the release of histamine and other chemicals that typically result in itchy skin (or paws, ears, face, armpits, and so on). These areas become reddened after the dog scratches or licks.

Signs of AD typically appear in dogs between ages six months and three years—with 75 percent of cases arising in dogs between the ages one and three. The disease occurs in both sexes, but some studies have reported higher incidence in females. AD often worsens during the summer, when pollen and mold levels increase. In about 75 percent of cases, the disease eventually becomes year-round.

Check with your vet, who will first rule out other skin disorders such as mange, ringworm, hookworm, and food allergies by performing skin scrapings, bacterial and fungal cultures, fecal analysis, and dietary trials. Subsequent tests may confirm AD. Approximately 90 percent of affected dogs give a positive immediate skin reaction, depending on the allergen. Intradermal skin tests are AD's only accurate diagnostic tool.

There's no real cure for allergies, but several treatment options ranging from avoidance to special shampoos and oils to medications may help. The most desirable treatment—and least practical—is to avoid the allergen. (Westies do not do well in "plastic bubbles.") Steroids such as prednisone are often effective in the short term. Antihistamines work well in some cases. The disease is clearly genetic, but its exact mode of inheritance has not been discovered.

Copper Toxicosis (CT)

Copper toxicosis (CT), a disease that can affect Westies, is due to an inborn glitch in copper metabolism that allows copper to accumulate in the liver, resulting in cirrhosis. Untreated, it is fatal.

The disease is usually well advanced before the first clinical signs appear. As copper continues to accumulate, widespread liver deterioration occurs, from which the dog can sometimes recover. He may lose weight and exhibit listlessness, anorexia, vomiting, abdominal pain, and jaundice. Eventually, cirrhosis occurs after continued loss of liver cells, and he may develop fluid in the abdominal cavity, causing death. Onset of clinical signs varies greatly but usually occurs in dogs four years of age or older.

The goal is to reduce the amount of copper deposited in the liver by using one of two medications. Both have effected positive results. Already approved for human use, another, zinc acetate, is also cheaper and being evaluated for FDA approval for canine application. Any treatment for CT should be administered only under veterinary supervision. The mode of inheritance remains undetermined for Westies. CT has been reported in at least 21 other breeds.

Craniomandibular Osteopathy (CMO)

Craniomandibular osteopathy (CMO—or "lion jaw") is a noncancerous growth of bone on the lower jaw. It usually affects both sides, but not always. Inflammation is the earliest symptom. You may notice the condition when a puppy shows discomfort while chewing or when you attempt to examine his mouth. So-called silent cases (where the pup appears unfazed) exist. Casual examination may not reveal an enlarged or abnormal jaw.

Most often recognized between the ages of four and seven months, it can occur as early as three to four weeks and, rarely, as late as nine to ten months. Experienced breeders and veterinarians usually recognize it before four months either by clinical signs or by palpation. X-rays of the skull and jaw will confirm CMO.

CMO is treatable. Depending on its severity, the amount of medication and length of treatment vary. (Four to ten months is the average length of treatment.) Many affected puppies will require some dose of cortisone until they are

CMO Facts

A simple recessive gene causes CMO: Both parents must carry at least one gene for it (i.e., they are "carriers" or, in the case of a recovered affected dog bred, "affected carriers"). Although studies on Westies, Scotties, and Cairns are in full swing in attempt to isolate the rogue gene, the birth of an affected puppy provides the only method of confirming both parents as carriers. Dr. Patrick Venta is working diligently to complete a map of the canine genome and isolate the genetic marker to help to develop a test for CMO.

ten months old or older. Most anti-inflammatory drugs work well, but since CMO may necessitate long-term therapy, veterinary advice is essential. Mild cases require little more than baby aspirin. Puppies nearly always recover. After therapy, the jaw remodels, and by the time the dog is two or three years old, it may be impossible to detect that he ever had the disease.

Ear Infections

Ear infections can be serious. Clean your Westie's ears with a canine ear cleaner on a regular basis. Check ears weekly to ensure the absence of infection or dark discharge. Keep hair out of the ear canals; trim hair from the ear tips about an inch down. Less hair weight puts less pressure on the ear cartilage. If infections occur, your vet may recommend a multipurpose antibacterial ointment. Chronic infections of the ear canal require prolonged treatment.

Yeast or fungal infections, common in Westies, indicate the need for an "ear culture." These conditions require treatment different from those for bacterial infections. Monitor ear infections closely and report hearing changes to your vet immediately.

Epidermal Dysplasia

Epidermal dysplasia (Westie armadillo syndrome) begins with reddening and itching of the skin, especially on the feet, legs, and the ventral parts of the body. The disease will intensify, with widespread redness developing. Hair loss and chronic inflammatory changes enter the picture. Eventually the dog's skin becomes thick and turns black, greasy, and foul smelling, which gave rise to the nickname Westie armadillo syndrome. Generalized severe itching worsens.

Armadillo syndrome can appear in pups as young as a few weeks to a few months of age. Both sexes are affected. This condition does not respond well to treatment, although there are two forms of the disease. In one, all treatment fails; in the other, high doses of systemic corticosteroids for a short period of time often bring a favorable response. Allow reasonable treatment time for possible recovery before euthanasia becomes necessary. How it's passed on remains undetermined. Although this condition does occur in this breed, cases are relatively uncommon.

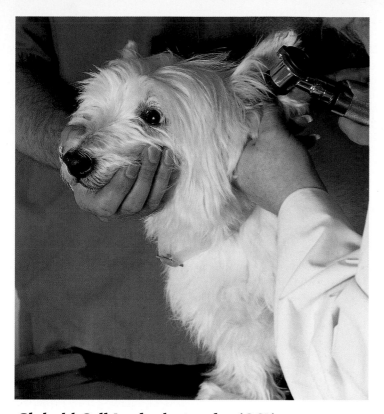

Ear infections can be serious, so it's important to check your Westie's ears weekly.

Globoid Cell Leukodystrophy (GCL)

Globoid cell leukodystrophy (GCL, or Krabbe's disease in humans) is a degenerative disease of the brain and spinal cord. It occurs from a lack of myelin, a necessary lipid that coats the spinal cord and other nerves. It's the result of a genetic deficiency of an enzyme (galactocerebroside b-galactosidase) involved in the breakdown of certain fats in the brain and spinal cord.

Symptoms begin early in life and progress rapidly and include weakness, stumbling, loss of control of the hindquarters, and tail tremors. Then the dog will develop a wide stance, lack of coordination, and posterior or total limb paralysis. He may become blind or fail to recognize familiar individuals. GCL may occur as early as four weeks of age and nearly always occurs before five or six months of age. The typical clinical signs and measurement of the mean activity of galactocerebroside b-galactosidase in white blood cells will confirm a positive diagnosis.

No treatment exists; GCL is fatal. Most common in Westies and Cairns, the disease is known to be a simple (autosomal) recessive.

Your Westie's Immune System

A dog's immune system is complex and confusing, and it operates at many levels. When all systems are working properly, a dog will resist infections, develop good immunity from vaccinations, and destroy tumor cells. When attacked by disease bacteria or tetanus toxin, the immune system will produce antibodies or antitoxins to fight them off or neutralize them, protecting the dog in the process.

Autoimmune diseases occur as a result of tissue injury caused by a specific immune reaction of the host to its own tissues. Since the immune system carries a diverse set of components, the clinical signs are complex as well. When it falls out of kilter, disease and allergies emerge. In autoimmune diseases the body can attack its own tissues, kidney, liver, and joints. Recent years have brought a large increase in liver disease to the canine population. Allergies are also on the increase. Blood work and a complete chemistry profile is the first step when immunity problems are suspected.

Progress and research in the treatment of several autoimmune diseases show promise. Allergies are not usually life threatening, but other autoimmune diseases can be quite serious. However, the potential for discomfort and severe debility is significant. Gaining control of allergies through diet is becoming popular: New innovative treatments are on the horizon.

Although many believe that autoimmune diseases have environmental origins, a genetic component is being researched. The Westie is susceptible to allergies and to other autoimmune diseases. Heed feeding and vaccine protocols for your Westie, as these may also be triggers.

Fortunately, an accurate blood test (using DNA technology) is now available to concerned breeders. It can accurately identify a dog as a carrier, as affected, or as clear of the disease. Testing a small blood sample identifies "carriers," whose offspring have a 50 percent chance of carrying the gene, but who will themselves be clear.

Breeders should test any dog in their breeding program to determine whether or not he's a carrier. This important tool is an opportunity to minimize the number of carriers in the Westie population and eventually eliminate GCL altogether. Dr. David Wenger, who developed the test for GCL in dogs, is currently working on developing a gene "fix" for affected children.

Inflammatory Bowel Disease (IBD)

Inflammatory bowel disease (IBD) is a condition of the dog's digestive system that involves the stomach, small intestine, and/or large intestine. According to Dr. Kay McGuire, a breeder/ exhibitor for 30 years (18 of which were with Westies) and veterinary consultant to the WHWTCA Health Committee, this condition's cause remains unknown.

In IBD, the dog's digestive tract is hypersensitive to foreign agents present in the bowel and its mucous membranes. Parasites, bacteria, dietary constituents, and drugs have all been suspects as possible causes of the condition. Chronic small bowel diarrhea, weight loss, flatulence, and foul-smelling stools characterize this syndrome. Vomiting is another sign seen in IBD. If symptoms remain chronic, large bowel diarrhea, halitosis, and anorexia may develop.

The most common initial tests a vet runs on a dog who is vomiting and having diarrhea are fecal flotation and stained fecal smears, which the vet evaluates for parasites. To be prudent, the vet commonly deworms the dog regardless of whether evidence of parasites exists. (Whipworms are notoriously hard to detect, so if they are the problem the dewormer will handle them.)

Food antigens can trigger IBD, especially in Westies. The veterinarian may suggest you switch your dog to a food whose protein and carbohydrates come from a different

Westies are generally considered a healthy, hardy breed.

source than his current food. There is also support for immune stimulation using a raw natural diet—efficacious in some cases, though questionable in others. After four to eight weeks, depending upon whether this effects any positive change, further diagnostic tests may be appropriate.

Kidney Disease

Renal (kidney) disease and renal failure are two distinct problems. Renal disease represents any degree of structural or functional kidney abnormality. It may be mild or extensive and progressive, resulting in kidney failure. Renal failure is the condition characterized by inability of the kidneys to excrete wastes and to help maintain the balance of electrolytes. This usually occurs when about 75 percent of normal renal function is lost, and will eventually have a deleterious effect on many other organs in the body.

Renal failure, whether associated with hereditary disease or with other causes, manifests identical symptoms. Rapid onset of symptoms is typical, even when the disease has been latent for quite some time. Owners report loss of appetite, excessive thirst and urination, depression, vomiting, and diarrhea. Bad breath, gum and tongue ulcers, anemia, dehydration, stunted growth, and loose teeth characterize kidney disease in immature dogs.

In addition to a complete blood count and chemistry profile, urinalysis provides valuable diagnostic information. X-rays reveal the size and shape of the kidneys, and a needle biopsy of the kidney will determine the extent of renal disease, to monitor its progression.

Treatment is directed toward delaying ultimate renal failure.

Hereditary kidney diseases are significant causes of kidney failure in young dogs of many breeds. Varieties of structural and/or functional defects may account for this disorder. How it's inherited remains vague, but research is in full swing. Recognizing the disease and removing Westies who manifest or produce pups with the disorder from breeding programs are the only ways of eliminating this type of genetic trait.

Legg-Calve-Perthes Disease

Legg-Calve-Perthes disease, also known as Legg-Perthes, refers to the "death" of the femoral head in one or both legs. An interruption of the blood supply to the femoral head results in the death and fracturing of bone cells. New bone growth and the remodeling of the femoral head and neck follow and lead to stiffness and pain in the rear leg or legs. Painful arthritis of the joint may occur.

In some cases, trauma, such as a fracture, can initiate the disorder. Sudden onset may also occur after the dog jumps off furniture. Other speculative predisposing causes are inflammation, nutritional factors, hip dysplasia, circulatory problems, and—possibly—excessive hormone production. Although specific causes of the disease are unknown, its mode of inheritance appears to be genetic, with trauma's only role being that of a trigger. Legg-Perthes can occur from three to eleven months of age.

Irritability and intermittent lameness that progresses to chronic hind-end lameness characterize its onset. As the disease progresses, the dog may exhibit pain when the leg is flexed. In severe cases, the dog becomes totally lame and avoids using the affected leg. The leg muscles begin to atrophy after extended periods of nonuse. Mild cases can be asymptomatic. X-rays provide the only certain method of diagnosis.

There's no specific treatment, although many vets prefer nonsurgical therapy: limiting activity, and treatment with nonsteroidal anti-inflammatory drugs for one month. If ineffective, surgical removal of the femur head eases pain and helps restore some function. Some dogs recover reasonable function without treatment.

The prognosis is generally excellent, and within several months the dog can again walk and run. In some cases, the affected leg may remain slightly shorter and the muscles may atrophy somewhat. Increased risk of arthritis, as the dog ages, is likely. Responsible breeders exclude Westies with Legg-Perthes—and those who have produced it—from their breeding programs. This polygenic trait arises in several small breeds of dogs.

OFA

The Orthopedic Foundation for Animals (OFA) has supported development of diagnostic criteria and databases for a number of genetic diseases, including Legg-Perthes, hip dysplasia, copper toxicosis, and luxating patella (www.offa.org).

Luxating Patella

The patella is the kneecap; *luxation* means "dislocation." Therefore, luxating patella is a dislocation of the kneecap. Other terms are "slipped kneecap," "slipped patella," or "slipped stifle." The kneecap protects the front of the stifle joint, which corresponds to the human knee joint. Anchored by ligaments, the patella fits in a groove in the femur.

Predisposing conditions to dislocation include shallow trochlear grooves, weak ligaments, and/or misalignment of the tendons and muscles that straighten the joint, so the patella slips inward or outward. It can occur in either one or both knees and may cause severe pain. It is inherited or acquired through trauma. With some small dogs, an isolated incident such as jumping off the couch can cause dislocation. No one has yet determined its exact mode of inheritance.

In severe cases, pain or lameness may lead to limping. Sometimes the slipped kneecap slips back into place. Manipulating the stifle joint and pushing the kneecap in and out of position can confirm diagnosis. X-rays to examine the trochlear ridges may help determine prognosis. Treatment consists of slipping the patella back into place, but relapses can occur. Surgery can repair the problem and may be the best option in the most severe cases.

Portosystemic Shunt

The liver filters blood from the digestive tract and stores energy. Portosystemic shunt (PSS) is an abnormal blood flow between the portal vein and a systemic vein that diverts blood from the liver into the general circulatory system. This allows blood from the intestine to bypass the liver. Toxins are not removed or metabolized from the circulation, resulting in neurological symptoms that appear gradually and may include episodic weakness, head pressing, disorientation, circling, pacing, behavioral changes, blindness, seizures, and coma. These often develop within minutes of a dog eating.

Most portosystemic shunts are congenital; they are most common in terriers. Affected animals may have a history of stunted growth or failure to gain weight. Definitive diagnosis of PSS is usually made by one year of age, and many puppies develop symptoms by four weeks of age. PSS tends to run in families but is believed to be polygenetic in nature, so research poses many challenges.

An ammonia tolerance test is the most reliable diagnostic tool to determine this hepatic abnormality. X-ray imaging studies where contrast dyes are injected into the liver will further confirm diagnosis. However, blood chemistry profile results can be normal. Many cases can be treated by partial surgical closure of the shunt. Dietary management may benefit dogs not treated surgically, but management is only palliative.

Pulmonary Fibrosis

We know very little about pulmonary fibrosis. Idiopathic pulmonary fibrosis (Westie Lung Disease) is a scarring and fibrosing of the lungs' air sacs and connective tissue. The scarring may result from chronic inflammation of the air sacs and can replace much of the normal structure of the lungs. (A similar disorder exists in humans.)

Its cause is unknown, as research has barely begun. However, some veterinary researchers suspect links between pulmonary fibrosis, the immune system, and allergies. Westies are more prone to pulmonary fibrosis than other breeds.

Other diseases can mimic its symptoms, so vets need to

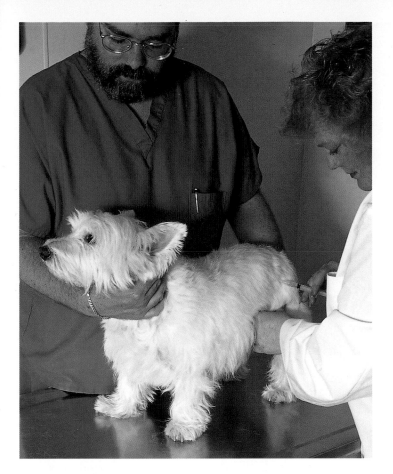

Yearly checkups are essential for keeping your Westie in tip-top shape.

be cautious when diagnosing pulmonary fibrosis. Following are some signs to look for when diagnosing pulmonary fibrosis; a Westie may not exhibit all of them:

- rapid shallow breathing or labored breathing
- loss of exercise tolerance
- scar tissue build-up in the lungs
- crackles in the lungs
- dry cough
- pulmonary hypertension or enlargement of the heart (due to breathing patterns)

Correct diagnosis is requires a lung biopsy. A tricky procedure in normal patients, lung biopsy may be quite risky in affected dogs. Furthermore, since many lung diseases exist, differentiation is difficult. Since so few samples have been taken, pathologist competence varies in interpreting these samples.

X-rays may reveal changes in the lungs, and abnormal blood gas levels may show lack of oxygen delivery to the tissues. A specialized machine can effectively screen people for

Exercise can do wonders for the health of your dog.

a similar disease; the machine is presently being tested on a control group of Westies.

Few treatment options exist. Once scarring occurs, little can be done. Preventing respiratory tract infections, limiting exercise, and incorporating planned weight loss for overweight Westies are all important. Bronchial dilating drugs may strengthen respiratory muscles, but Westies tend to develop tolerance, and the medicine loses its efficacy. Some dogs may benefit from controlled use of steroids, such as Prednisone and Interferon. Experimental usage of inhaled steroids has been tried in some cases, and cough suppressants can alleviate some discomfort.

The prognosis is very poor. Lung disease appears to affect older Westies, with the average age of onset about nine years. After diagnosis, most patients survive an average of 17 to 24 months. Recently, veterinary respiratory specialists formed an international study group, which should help speed research.

Pyruvate Kinase Deficiency (PK)

Pyruvate kinase (PK) deficiency (erythrocyte pyruvate kinase deficiency) in red blood cells (erythrocytes) causes a severe hemolytic (red cell rupture) anemia as a result of the premature destruction of PK-deficient red blood cells.

PK is an enzyme in glycolysis, which is essential for the metabolism of glucose into an energy source utilized by cells such as red blood cells. Without this source of energy, red blood cells are unable to function properly and are consequently destroyed.

The clinical signs of anemia are very pale mucous membranes (gums), increased heart rate and pounding pulses, weakness, and exercise intolerance. The liver and spleen may be enlarged, and after one year of age, the density of all bones, particularly long bones and the skull, appear increased. Well-confined affected dogs may not show any obvious signs but may acutely decompensate and die when severely exercised or stressed.

After excluding the more common causes of hemolytic anemia—autoimmune, toxic, and infectious hemolytic anemia, PK deficiency should be considered. A chronic, severe, highly regenerative hemolytic anemia associated with increased radiographic bone density in older animals suggests of PK deficiency, which is diagnosed through DNA analysis. A simple determination of PK activity will not diagnose an affected dog, but it does allow the detection of carriers.

There is no simple treatment. When large iron deposition occurs in tissues, treatment may include chelation. At least in research, bone marrow transplant shows potential for curing the disease. Affected dogs usually die young (one to four years) due to progressive anemia or liver failure.

Seborrhea

Seborrhea is a skin disorder that can appear in either primary or secondary forms. Therapy depends largely upon which of the two forms the dog manifests; so it is necessary to distinguish between them. Primary seborrhea is idiopathic—it exists by itself. This form, which occurs in Westies and some other breeds, most often appears in young animals and is generally thought to have a genetic component.

Primary seborrhea is characterized by symptoms of this disease alone. A trained dermatologist should rule out all other causes. Symptoms include scaly, oily patches adhering to the skin. Since the oil collects dirt, it's sometimes called dirty puppy disease. Abrasions tend to be more severe on elbows, hocks, and ears. Typically, lesions are hairless, dark centered, scaly patches surrounded by a reddened area and flaking; they typically occur on the trunk and chest.

Secondary seborrhea, which arises primarily in adults, occurs if the signs are associated with an underlying disease indirectly related to the seborrhea itself. Endocrine disorders like hypothyroidism or hypoadrenocorticism can trigger the secondary form. Nutritional disorders, especially those involving fat, can be a root cause. Parasites, drug hypersensitivity, local trauma, tumors, and any chronic catabolic state may also cause secondary seborrhea. Although secondary seborrhea resembles primary seborrhea, treatment of secondary seborrhea heavily depends on the cause of the problem.

Primary seborrhea is a chronic condition: It must be managed since it cannot be cured. Medicated shampoos and some ointments containing tar, salicylic acid, and sulfur can relieve symptoms. Systemic and topical corticosteroids may help. Systemic antibiotics, vitamin A, and retinoids have netted good results.

Skin Allergy Problems

Skin problems are usually caused by an allergic reaction to something in the environment—whether it's fleas, mold, dust, pollen, grass, food, or chemicals—that causes a dog to itch and leads to scratching. Constant scratching may cause a breakdown in the skin that leads to bacterial infection—and the problem.

We cannot rid all allergens from a dog's environment, but we can control some—we can eliminate fleas, adjust diet, and boost the immune system. One flea can wreak havoc on a dog with a flea allergy.

The next very important issue is dealing with infection. If your dog has one or more of the following symptoms, you may have to treat for secondary bacterial infection:

- hair loss
- scaling, flaky skin
- open sores
- greasy skin and coat
- thick black skin
- pimples
- moist, puffy skin
- chronic ear infection
- odor
- red swollen feet and pads

Antibiotics may actually cure the infection; treatment length is dependant upon how long your Westie has had symptoms. Chronic cases require oral antibiotic treatment anywhere from two to six weeks, in addition to topical treatment. The type of antibiotic used is extremely important. Keep the skin clean whenever treating skin infections. The type of shampoo prescribed and the frequency of bathing depend upon the symptoms. Medicated cornstarch and zinc both heal and soothe the skin.

The use of prednisone to treat skin conditions remains controversial. Considered for years the only way to treat the chronic allergy/skin condition, this has been proved untrue. Prednisone may be used in combination with other therapies for skin problems—with caution. Steroids suppress the immune system. Furthermore, prednisone does not cure the skin infection; it merely provides temporary relief. Antihistamines relieve the itching associated with allergic reactions and present fewer risks than steroids.

Improper diet can cause some allergies. Many vets recommend a change—perhaps to a high-quality lamb and rice diet formula exclusive of soy, wheat, corn, beet pulp, fillers, beef products, animal by-products, and preservatives. Fish and potato foods are another option, or you may choose to prepare your Westie's food or feed a raw natural diet. The West Highland White Terrier Club of America website (www.westieclubofamerica.com) includes information on other dietary options that have worked for many Westie owners.

Supplementing with vitamins C, E, zinc, and omega-3 and -6 fatty acids may help restore the body to a healthy state. These supplements come in all-in-one gel capsules. Owners have found that adding digestive enzymes to the diet of dogs with compromised immune systems can be beneficial.

Not all skin problems are allergy generated. It is easy to assume that the Westie's problem is

allergies. Underlying thyroid condition, dog lice, and sarcoptic or demodetic mange mites can cause similar symptoms. For proper diagnosis, your vet may recommend blood tests, skin scrapings, or biopsies.

Responsible breeding helps cut down on many diseases that can affect Westies.

White Shaker Dog Syndrome

This syndrome is a unique generalized tremor that occurs in young, predominately small dogs. Because this syndrome was initially seen in larger numbers of dogs with white coats, it is called white shaker dog syndrome (WSS).

Dogs with WSS have a fine tremor of the entire body. Young dogs (nine months to three years old) are most frequently affected. The tremor usually persists throughout the day and worsens with handling, excitement, or stress. Without therapy, the magnitude of the tremor may increase or remain constant. Other occasional clinical signs include head tilts, limb weakness, and seizures.

The disease is most often associated with a mild central nervous system inflammation, which commonly affects the brain's cerebellum; its dysfunction may initiate the tremor. Some veterinarians believe that its cause is an underlying virus, but no research supports this theory, nor has any infectious basis been found. Whether the inflammation is really the source of the tremor or whether some other associated neurotransmitter abnormality results in this abnormal firing of nerves is unknown.

WSS diagnosis is based on clinical symptoms alone. Lab tests and physical exams are usually normal. The disease, though rarely fatal, can be very disturbing.

WSS is characterized by a sudden onset of constant tremors all over the body, including the head and eyeballs, with chaotic random eye movement and rapid, involuntary, rhythmic eye movement of a type that often indicates central nervous system dysfunction. The tremors are exacerbated by handling, forced locomotion, excitement, and high levels of stress, and decrease but may not completely disappear with total relaxation. Putting the dog in a crate in a minimally darkened, quiet room may help reduce the tremors, which may be severe enough to cause an uncoordinated gait during stressful periods. Occasionally a dog convulses. Usually for a short time at the onset, he refuses to eat. If you can't gently coax your Westie to eat or drink, you will have to hand-feed him. Eventually, he'll return to eating and drinking on his own. Elevating his food and water bowls may be helpful so that he does not have to lower his head to eat.

Supportive therapy includes reducing the tremors with diazepam and anti-inflammatory drugs (corticosteroids), but neither alone is rapidly or consistently effective. According to veterinary neurologist, Dr. Alan Parker, using both drugs simultaneously has been the most effective and reliable. Early diagnosis is beneficial, as many dogs will respond in a few days to immunosuppressive levels of corticosteroids. Some dogs need maintenance on low levels of these drugs for several months, but others never require them. Do not decrease the corticosteroid dose too quickly.

The duration of therapy is critical; ending therapy prematurely usually leads to a relapse. This simultaneous dual-drug treatment can cause symptoms to decrease as quickly as the second day. By the fifth day, dogs are usually 80 percent normal.

OTHER COMMON CANINE DISEASES

Arthritis

Arthritis is an inflammation of the joint. It may be associated with any combination of swelling, pain, fluid accumulation, cartilage degeneration, or bone proliferation.

While mild arthritis is uncomfortable, severe arthritis is very painful. Symptoms of osteoarthritis in your Westie might include stiffness in the joints, limb favoring, difficulty in sitting or standing, hesitancy to jump, decreased activity level, irritability, aggression, and lethargy.

Several treatments exist for pain management for canine arthritis, but there is no cure. Your vet may also prescribe medication to reduce inflammation and discomfort. But if using these in the long term, make sure you monitor your Westie for side effects—especially liver damage.

Newer treatment appears in the nutraceuticals glucosamine and chondroitin. These can help relieve inflammation and even delay the degenerative process in some dogs. By attracting fluid to the joint's remaining cartilage system, the body may repair damaged joints while keeping the cartilage-destroying enzymes in check. They show promise as a preventative measure for dogs with high risk factors for arthritis.

Other alternative therapies, such as acupuncture, Chinese medicine, and herbs have provided many dogs with relief. Personal experience treating one of my dogs with these has yielded amazing results.

Cancer

Cancer is a general term for more than 200 different types of malignancies that can affect the body. What they have in common is "modus operandi": they result from accelerated cell growth; the cells are all "undifferentiated," meaning that they can no longer be recognized as a cell from a particular organ. In a cruel irony, unlike normal cells that are born and die, cancer cells reproduce indefinitely.

Many factors may initiate cancers, but scientists believe that hormones may play a prominent role, especially in cancers of the reproductive system and thyroid. Hormones can stimulate abnormal cells to divide and develop into tumors.

Age, type of cancer, cure rate, and even personality type can help determine the best treatment. Be sure to discuss all options with your veterinarian. Costs can also vary widely, ranging from little more than an average surgery to your life's savings.

Diabetes Mellitus

Diabetes mellitus, often called sugar diabetes, strikes dogs as well as humans. This endocrine disease results from a

Signs of Cancer

The Veterinary Cancer Society (www.vetcancersociety.org) lists the following common signs of cancer in small animals:

- abnormal swellings that persist or continue to grow
- sores that don't heal
- weight loss
- loss of appetite
- bleeding or discharge from any body opening
- offensive odor
- difficulty eating or swallowing
- hesitation to exercise or loss of stamina
- persistent lameness or stiffness
- difficulty breathing, urinating, or defecating

deficiency in the pancreas's production of the hormone insulin.

This disease occurs most frequently in overweight dogs six to nine years of age and is more common among intact females. There may be a genetic propensity for diabetes. It is noncurable and ultimately affects all organs. Its cause remains unknown, and many dogs develop it in conjunction with other disorders.

Symptoms include increased appetite and water consumption, increased frequency and volume of urination, and weight loss. In more advanced cases, lethargy, loss of appetite, vomiting, dehydration, weakness, and coma may occur. Veterinarians diagnose based on history, physical examination, and laboratory test results: urinalysis and blood sugar levels and other diagnostic tests.

With daily treatment, prognosis is good. Diet and exercise alone can control some mild cases. Others need more comprehensive management: daily insulin injections, urine testing, dietary management, regular exercise, and avoidance or control of concurrent illnesses. Most dogs require insulin injections twice a day to control blood glucose levels. Insulin requirements cannot be predicted solely on the basis of the dog's weight because the degree of pancreatic failure is different in each dog, so treatment must be individualized.

Obesity reduces the responsiveness to insulin, making diabetes more difficult to control. A specialized, gradual weight reduction plan will help your diabetic dog reach his ideal body weight. His weight and activity level determines his caloric intake. Feeding multiple small meals throughout the day minimizes risk of hypoglycemia; daily caloric consumption must remain consistent.

A diabetic Westie requires a strict insulin-injection schedule. Your vet may fine-tune treatment based on monitored test results. Oh, and cancel that stop at the donut shop you had planned. You'll both live longer and look better in a swimsuit.

Heart Disease

A congenital heart defect is present at birth. Acquired heart disease is that which develops after birth. Many dogs show no outward signs of heart disease; others exhibit weakness, exercise intolerance, coughing, labored breathing, poor growth, collapse, or have a blue tinge to the mouth's mucous membranes.

Heart disease can remain undetected until a veterinary exam is performed. Coordinate puppy examinations with their vaccine schedule and periodically check thereafter. The vet may discover congenital heart defects by listening for a heart murmur, which is classified according to loudness, location, and timing in the cardiac cycle. Innocent or flow murmurs, not uncommon in puppies, are not loud and generally disappear by four to six months of age. However, if physical examination suggests a cardiac anomaly, you vet will perform tests such as an electrocardiogram and radiographs to assess severity. A yearly checkup is good preventative care for all dogs. Carefully monitor your older Westie.

Treatment varies according to each case. Some dogs need medication; others require surgical intervention or a pacemaker. Congenital heart defects may be inherited or may develop during gestation for unknown reasons or after exposure to toxins.

Pancreatitis

The pancreas produces enzymes (needed to digest food) and hormones, including insulin. Pancreatitis occurs when the organ starts leaking those enzymes and actually starts digesting itself. Some types are sudden and acute; others develop over time. Both kinds are life threatening.

Pancreatitis is notoriously difficult to diagnose. Risk factors can include abnormally high fat content in the blood, obesity, infection, or contaminated food. Other diseases such as diabetes and even some drugs have been known to trigger it. A high-fat meal just before the onset of the disease is also common.

Symptoms may include vomiting, appetite loss, changes in body temperature (either way) and a painful abdomen. Diarrhea and depression are also common; so is dehydration. Your vet will run tests including a check on the pancreatic enzymes for more clues. Sometimes X-rays are required.

The only treatment is supportive therapy, usually feeding through IVs for a few days in order to rest the digestive system. A low-fat diet is a likely prescription for your recovering Westie.

Steer Clear of Fast Food

Avoid feeding your Westie French fries and other fast-foods. You don't want to "super-size" him or cause pancreatitis.

Check your Westie for fleas and ticks after he's been outside.

PARASITES

Parasites cause problems running the gamut from mild itching to death. External parasites include various mites, fleas, and ticks. Internal ones are usually worms like roundworm, hookworm, whipworm, and heartworm. Many of these can be prevented or controlled.

External Parasites

These are parasites that live on—but not inside—a dog's body. With the exception of some mites, they are visible.

Fleas

A female flea can lay 2,000 eggs in her lifetime. Despite this astonishing skill and the species' reputation for putting on circuses rivaling the Cirque de Soleil, many people aren't too keen on them. Perhaps this is because they are bloodsucking and nasty, cause your beloved Westie allergic reactions, and transmit tapeworm as an added bonus. Fleas bite people, too, although dogs are their eating establishments of choice.

Besides constant scratching, a sure of sign of fleas on your dog is the presence of blackish/reddish granules. These are flea feces, largely composed of your dog's blood.

Flea and tick preventatives come in two basic kinds: adulticides that kill adult fleas on contact, and insect growth regulators (IGR), which function like flea birth control: They interrupt their life cycle. They don't kill adult fleas, so it's more of a "community service" than a flea-bite preventative.

Mange, Demodectic (Demodex)

Demodectic mange, also called red mange or *Demodex*, is a fairly common skin disease. While the mite that is the catalyst, *Demodex canis*, is found on most dogs, only some seem to suffer adverse effects—likely due to a subpar or immature immune system. (Puppies are most commonly affected.) Demodectic mites crowd out the hair follicles, causing them to fall out. In addition, follicles often become infected and the skin red and inflamed. A skin scraping will confirm the diagnosis. Mange in puppies usually resolves itself but is often treated with insecticides.

Demodectic mange in an adult dog may indicate a weakened immune system. It is very serious and requires competent veterinary attention.

Mange, Sarcoptic (Scabies)

Sarcoptic mange, or scabies, a highly contagious parasitic disease, affects susceptible humans and dogs—and livestock. The "perpetrator" is a tiny mite called *Sarcoptes scabiei* that burrows in the skin to cause itchiness, redness, and hair loss in both people and dogs. Treatment for scabies includes an arsenal of special shampoos, dips, pills, and injections.

Ticks

Although a tick or two doesn't seem to cause any discomfort to the affected dog the way a flea infestation does, all 850 species can be dangerous. They carry quite an array of diseases, including the most notorious: Lyme disease, Rocky Mountain spotted fever, and tick paralysis.

If you discover a tick on your dog, pull it off with a pair of fine-tipped tweezers. Wear gloves if possible. Grip it as close to the head as possible to avoid crushing it. Once removed, toss it into some alcohol to kill it. Disinfect the site of the bite and wash your hands. Bite wounds may develop into welts from the tick's saliva but should heal in about a week.

Internal Parasites

Worms are disturbing parasites that affect both puppies and adult dogs. There are dozens of varieties. Different species

Flea Facts

Fleas can jump 150 times their own length, accelerate faster than a cheetah, and survive without food for up to a year! All this without anabolic steroids!

can infect different parts of the dog's body. Some kinds attack the esophagus and stomach; others go for the small intestine (roundworms, hookworms, threadworms, trichina worms, tapeworms, and flukes). Still others, like whipworm, target the colon. Almost every organ can be prey to some kind of worm: liver, nasal cavity, trachea, lungs, heart, kidney, nervous system, arteries, and veins. Some worms are transmitted though food. Freezing meat to minus 40°F (4°C) for two days or heating it to 140°F (60°C) kills them. Unless you live in a meat locker or have a few tanks of liquid nitrogen handy, this could prove impractical. Some worms can transmit diseases to people. Hookworms, in particular, are a real public-health concern.

You can keep your dog worm-free by using a regular dewormer (many heartworm preventives work). Also keep your Westie's quarters and your yard clean.

Heartworm

Heartworms are wicked creatures that camp out in the right side of the heart, obstructing its large blood vessels. Badly infected dogs can have hundreds of these in their hearts for years. Heartworms lay tiny larvae in the bloodstream (microfilaria) that live for three years. Their offspring circulate in the bloodstream. Transmitted to other animals via mosquitoes, they enter a new host.

It takes six to seven months from the time an animal is bitten until the symptoms appear. These include coughing, fluid accumulation, decreased appetite, and heart failure. Reliable tests can detect infection. The disease, left untreated, is nearly always fatal. Furthermore, the treatment is risky, long, and difficult.

Monthly preventative tablets, available by prescription, will keep your Westie free of heartworm. A single mosquito bite can transmit heartworm, so play it safe (especially where mosquitoes fly rampant) and keep your dog on the preventative tablets. They work by immediately killing larvae acquired within the previous 30 days—but they won't kill adult worms. Heartworm medication also safeguards your Westie from hookworms, roundworms, and whipworms.

Hookworm

This unsavory critter latches on to the intestinal wall with its tiny teeth. Hookworms cause intestinal bleeding,

Heartworm Tip

If you live in the South, it's a good idea to keep your dog on a year round heartworm preventative.

pain, and anemia; just a few dozen of them can kill a puppy. They deposit their larvae where they can be easily picked up again—either through the skin or by mouth. They like shady, sandy areas best, so barefoot children are also at risk. Larvae can actually penetrate the skin and cause lesions. They leech out nutrients, causing malnutrition as well.

Ringworm

"Worm" is a misnomer for this disease. Ringworm is actually a highly contagious fungus dogs catch from each other—or from kids. More common in puppies than in adult dogs, classic signs include scabs, irregular-shaped skin infections, or hair loss at the site. Ringworm is very similar to many other skin problems, and the only definitive diagnosis is by culture. Since ringworm is contagious to people, you'll want to treat it with your vet's guidance. Your vet will clip the hair from around the affected areas and bathe the skin with a special shampoo; for more serious cases, a prescription may be required.

Roundworm

Nearly every puppy born comes with roundworms; it's one of their mother's first gifts. Roundworms penetrate the small intestine and travel through the bloodstream to the liver and lungs, and even up the trachea, where they are swallowed. This cycle perpetuates as they continue to produce eggs that are excreted with the feces. The worms can relocate to muscle tissue, form cysts, and go dormant. Though less likely to be infected, older dogs can pick up roundworms from contaminated soil.

Children playing in areas where dogs have defecated can get roundworm from placing dirty fingers in their mouths. Children with roundworms may be misdiagnosed as having contracted flu.

Whipworm

This is the most difficult of all worms to vanquish; whipworms' eggs seem impervious to time and cold weather, and a whipworm can lay 2,000 eggs a day. Severe infestations can give dogs horrendous cases of colitis.

Tapeworms

If you see something that looks like white rice in your Westie's feces, it's probably tapeworm. Dogs become infested by eating a flea with a tapeworm larvae. Tapeworm isn't as serious in dogs as it is in people, and a weight-appropriate dose of Droncit will eliminate it.

You might want to explore holistic medicine for your Westie.

HOLISTIC MEDICINE

The holistic approach to addressing disease and health refers to treating the patient as a whole organism rather than merely eliminating the symptoms of an isolated problem or part of the anatomy. It is, in the general sense, the least intrusive way to assist your dog to heal himself and regain his maximum level of health. Many alternative modalities address appropriate treatment for each individual animal. Holistic medicine can also dovetail with allopathic (conventional) medicine beautifully.

Illness indicates an imbalance within the body: A runny eye might indicate problems with the liver, or allergies might lead to chronic ear problems. Within the body, everything is connected. Strict allopathic (or Western) vets, when treating an ear infection, will help eliminate symptoms, but may not address the underlying cause. The holistic approach seeks to address the animal as a whole. Some proponents of holistic care believe that when only a symptom is relieved, the underlying problem simply burrows itself deeper within the body. However, these two approaches are not mutually exclusive. Obviously, allopathic medication and surgery will save lives when holistic remedies fall short.

Holistic medicine includes homeopathy, Chinese medicine, herbal supplementation, essential oils, acupuncture, and chiropractic, as well as other therapies.

Acupuncture

Acupuncture is an ancient Chinese art ideal for dogs with arthritis, hip dysplasia, and other muscular-skeletal issues. Dogs with cancer, allergies, and nervous and circulatory system issues have also reaped its benefits.

Acupuncture involves the gentle insertion of fine needles. Many dogs hardly seem to notice it or only experience slight discomfort. Electroacupuncture, where traditional needle acupuncture is combined with a microcurrent of electricity, has further refined the therapy. Why acupuncture works—especially to Westerners—is somewhat mysterious. Eastern acupuncturists believe it channels the flow of Chi, a Chinese word for "energy," through certain "body paths" known as meridians.

Western practitioners have noted that the sites of acupuncture usually have thinner skin than surrounding tissues and that each one contains a lymph vessel, arteriole, and vein, plus a bundle of nerve fibers. So the needles stimulate the central and automatic nervous systems, which release endorphins, diminishing the perception of pain. Other acupoints may release cortisol, a natural steroid. Whatever the explanation, personal experience with my own dog, who sustained injury-induced arthritis, has convinced me that it really does work.

Chiropractic Care

Dogs who develop bone and joint problems may benefit from veterinary chiropractic care.

As a supplement to conventional care, it may enhance its efficacy. Some veterinarians provide chiropractic; some vets are specialists, but each should have special training and a license from the American Veterinary Chiropractic Association.

The benefits of chiropractic care are many, but it's not a

Don't Give Up!

Westie breeder Christine Swingle had a Westie diagnosed with WSS at age three. Drugs worsened the situation to the point where she was forced to consider euthanizing him. After discontinuing the drugs, he began to eat and drink on his own. Today, when things get stressful, she isolates him in a quiet room for 15 minutes to half an hour. She has discovered, also, that Rescue Remedy helps him immensely during times of strain.

cure-all. It cannot cure hip or elbow dysplasia. However, by carefully manipulating vertebrae, it can help delay deterioration. Chiropractors examine for irregularities between vertebrae, and adjust them in order to restore spinal alignment. Chiropractic can benefit disk problems, may help prevent surgery, or can offer valuable aftercare. Even conformation dogs, obedience dogs, and canine athletes, like agility dogs, can benefit from a chiropractic "tune-up" to enhance performance.

Flower Essences

Edward Bach developed this branch of alternative medicine in England early in the 1900s. Today there are about 50,000 active practitioners worldwide. Although there are 38 different combinations of flower essences in Bach's pharmacopeias (and more than 200 other blends developed since), the most famous is Bach's special blend of five flower essences, produced and most commonly sold under the name Rescue Remedy, widely touted for its calming effect on nervous and stressed dogs.

The theory behind flower-essence therapy is called resonance, and healers caution that it works best when the essence you select matches the core emotional challenges the dog faces—if you can figure out what they are. The therapy is not designed to cure physical ailments but rather to aid in psychological and emotional problems than can develop into physical distress. Flower essences are usually preserved in brandy, but you can also use cider vinegar. (Mightn't a good single-malt scotch whiskey be more suited to Westies?)

Flower essences are usually administered in doses of four drops four times a day. These essences can be rubbed into the gums or added to some bread and fed to the dog. Flower-essence therapy requires frequent application, as its effects are transient. Holistic vets usually combine these with other kinds of therapy—particularly with herbs and essential oils.

Flower-essence therapy does nothing to worsen the condition, and many consider its effects just short of miraculous.

Herbal Therapy

Dog owners looking for alternatives to Western medications might consider herbal medicine. Traditional Chinese

Safety Tip

If you're not an expert, refrain from collecting herbal remedies in the wild. Also, some native plants are becoming extremely rare due to overcollection, so buy your herbs commercially and on the advice of an experienced practitioner.

medicine, Western herbalism, and Ayurvedic medicine, which originated in India and the Middle East, are all examples of herbal therapy. Each branch of herbal medicine has a slightly different emphasis, but all aim to encourage the body to maintain its own health. The focus is on wellness, whereas conventional Western medicine concentrates on the treatment of disease.

Since herbal medicine is complex, you increase your chances of getting good results by consulting a qualified veterinary herbalist. Many such practitioners are also DVMs who seek to expand treatment options for their clients.

Herbs are not a quick fix. In fact, most herbs act more slowly than potent drugs (many of which derive from them). Neither are herbs panaceas that will eliminate all your dog's health issues. Moreover, not every herb will work on every disease, and some diseases are simply incurable. Many herbs may lack the purity of laboratory-tested medications, so dosing may be trickier to get right.

These shortcomings, however, do not invalidate their value in veterinary medicine. They often alleviate pain and relieve symptoms. In fact, many have the same properties (not necessarily holistic, either) as conventional medications. Treating a symptom and treating the underlying condition won't necessarily call for the same herbal or drug regimen, and confused pet owners who mix the two modalities may get disappointing results.

Although herbal dosages vary from case to case, they are much more forgiving than are Western-style drugs. In most cases, you can administer doses to your pet roughly in proportion to the recommended human dose—that is, according to weight. However, since dogs' metabolic rates are higher than people's, dogs may require proportionately higher

initial dosages to reach therapeutic levels. To be safe, work this out with your animal herbalist.

Herbs act in a variety of ways, just as conventional medications do. Some help kill bacteria and fungi in the body. Others act as astringents and promote skin and bowel health. Some have sedative properties; others are diuretics. Herbs can support cardiovascular health, reduce inflammation, and promote optimal digestive system function. Others benefit the entire immune system and promote healing.

Herbal medications come in many forms. The dried, bulk form is useful because you can add some directly to your dog's food. Shelf life varies and depends on how it's preserved. Read labels carefully, and don't buy more than you will use.

Homeopathy

Homeopathy has become an important part of legitimate veterinary practice. Its use is about 200 years old, but it has been a part of folk medicine for centuries. Today there are 1,350 recognized homeopathic remedies. Many people dispute their efficacy, but others swear by them.

Homeopathy works on the simple principle that "like cures like." To cure an illness, you give the patient a very small diluted (attenuated) amount of a substance which, in large amounts, would produce symptoms similar to the target disease. In theory, the body responds by resetting its systems to heal itself. The major difference in philosophy between homeopathy and conventional Western medicine is that traditional medicine usually works by introducing a foreign substance into the body to treat the illness. Homeopaths believe that this can cause harm than by overloading the body with two problems instead of one.

The most curious thing about homeopathic remedies concerns the "potency" of the substance (not to be confused with the "strength" of a conventional drug). In homeopathy, the more dilute the substance is, the greater it potency. Very potent remedies have none of the original substance left in them, but they theoretically retain the "energy" from it. Pellets commonly come with numbers like 6C, 12C, or 30C. The higher the number, the more attenuated the substance, and the higher the potency. Without professional advice, *do not use anything above 30C, and always check with a homeo-*

pathic vet before administering remedies designed for humans to dogs. An "almost" right dose can be very wrong in homeopathy.

Homeopathy remedies are usually given one at time and should not be combined with conventional medicine, acupuncture, or herbal treatments. However, homeopathic remedies may be combined with flower-essence therapy. Massage, nutritional therapy, and chiropractic care also do not interfere. Opinions differ regarding acupressure.

All veterinary homeopaths are also DVMs. The have also completed 128 hours of instruction in approved courses, and passed two exams. The American Holistic Veterinary Medical Association lists its members at www.theavh.org.

Physical Therapy

Many dogs benefit from physical therapy after surgery or when plagued with a chronic condition. A canine physical therapist may be a veterinarian, licensed veterinary technician, or licensed human physical therapist with special training in canine therapy. Make sure a regular physical

Remember to stay calm during emergencies—your Westie is counting on you.

therapist certified to practice on animals will work in partnership with your vet for the best results.

Types and advantages of physical therapy include the following:

- *Hydrotherapy* improves range of motion and muscle strength, usually by means of the underwater treadmill. Some vets recommend swimming.
- *Therapeutic ultrasound* uses high-frequency sound waves to reduce pain and muscle spasms, enhance collagen production, increase blood flow, and speed healing.
- *Neuromuscular stimulation* uses electrical stimulation to help dogs regain muscle function and improve range of motion.
- *Passive range-of-motion* therapies involve manipulating the dog's limbs and joints to stimulate blood flow and increase range of motion in weakness or paralysis.
- *Therapeutic exercises* build muscle, recover balance, and strengthen the cardiovascular system.

FIRST AID AND OTHER EMERGENCIES

In any emergency, first take a deep, cleansing breath and try to stay calm. This will enable you to act rationally, and your Westie's life may depend on it. For instance, you just noticed that your Westie has eaten the entire population of your daughter's ant farm, and you are uncertain whether ants are toxic. (Most are not.) Call your vet or a poison control center and never act out of panic.

First Aid Supplies for Dogs

"A first aid kit can be as basic or as complete as you want to make it," suggests WHWTCA Corresponding Secretary and *AKC Gazette* Westie columnist, Nancy Staab. "Find an appropriate container—anything from a fanny pack to a larger zippered tote, and gather supplies."

The following are all useful and would cover just about any emergency:

- gauze sponges
- self-adhering bandages
- petroleum jelly
- hydrogen peroxide
- rubbing alcohol (a good cleaning agent)
- antacids that combine with stomach acid to neutralize it

- Benadryl (use the children's liquid)
- triple antibiotic ointment
- hydrocortisone acetate 1% (ointment or cream)
- buffered aspirin
- Kaopectate tablets
- cold pack
- stainless steel hemostat or kelly forceps (wonderful multipurpose tools)
- digital thermometer dedicated to dog use
- adhesive tape (I prefer the cotton athletic tape.)
- pair of EMT (utility) scissors
- blanket
- tweezers
- muzzle
- zip-type plastic bags
- paperwork, including your Westie's health records, medications, local and national poison control numbers, regular veterinary clinic hours and telephone numbers, and emergency clinic hours and telephone number

Temerature Tip

Take your dog's temperature several times, so that you will know his normal temperature. Record it and store the piece of paper and the thermometer in a zip-type plastic bag. Most dogs' normal temperature is around 101°F (38°C).

Heatstroke

Heatstroke can occur any time the temperature rises above 70°F (21°C). Dogs perspire through the pads of their feet, which is not all that efficient. Their only other method of heat exchange, panting, allows them to move large volumes of warm air outside their bodies. Westies are hardly tropical animals, so heat and humidity can be perilous.

Access to cool, fresh water and a well-shaded haven, especially outdoors, help prevent heatstroke. Never leave your Westie outside in the hot sun, and confine exercise periods to the cooler parts of the day or to evenings. Some Westies really enjoy a small children's wading pool. Others love hose play and leap in ecstasy after the water plumes.

Signs of heatstroke include panting, weakness, and loss of coordination. Gums may appear gray or dark red instead of healthy pink. Vomiting, diarrhea, seizures, and death may follow. If you suspect heatstroke, drench you Westie with cool (not cold) water. If his body temperature rises above 105°F (40°C), he will need hospitalization and intravenous fluids. Such elevated temperatures prevent sufficient oxygen from reaching tissues and can cause brain damage.

Many plants are poisonous, so keep an eye on your Westie while he is outside.

Insect Stings

Unless your Westie has a serious allergic reaction, treat bee stings with liquid or capsule Benadryl. If his breathing becomes labored, however, he may be having an allergic reaction; promptly get him to the vet. (One of my dogs eats bees like candy—I am fortunate that he is not allergic to them.)

Moving an Injured Dog

The best way to move your injured dog depends upon the nature of the injury. If possible, muzzle him beforehand. Even the gentlest dog can bite when injured and frightened. With a suspected back or neck injury, gently slide him onto a board. This reduces the possibility of further injury. In case of other types of injuries, carry him, cradle his body, and wrap him in a blanket. Hold the injured side against your body. You might also carry him in a box or pet carrier.

Poisoning

So many plants, drugs, and cleaning products are poisonous to dogs that it's impossible to list them all. However, you can find a comprehensive listing of toxic plants and other vital information at www.aspca.org/toxicplants/M01947.htm.

If you suspect your Westie has been poisoned, immediately call your vet and/or the ASPCA National Animal Poison Control Center at 1-900-443-0000 (a fee is charged per case). The charge is billed directly to the caller's phone. Don't hesitate to call because of the fee: Your dog's life is at stake and the organization is nonprofit. You'll be talking to a real veterinarian, and you'll get extremely fast, life-saving advice.

Wounds and Bleeding

If the wound is comparatively minor (no major bleeding), first remove debris and any foreign objects stuck in the wound. If you have clippers, cut the hair away from the wound site, and clean the area with a cleansing solution. Soap works, too. Avoid hydrogen peroxide, which can damage the tissue. If bleeding is profuse, you may be looking at a life-threatening situation that requires veterinary attention. To control bleeding, apply direct pressure with a clean bandage and, if possible, raise the bleeding portion above the rest of the body.

YOUR VENERABLE WESTIE

For Westies, the onset of old age is somewhat variable: the aging process begins somewhere between ages seven and ten. Proper health measures can help stave off the aging process. Older dogs should have an annual physical to evaluate all systems. This exam might include a baseline blood work panel, urinalysis, and fecal check, with other tests as needed.

Vision and hearing are primary concerns as your Westie ages. Older Westies may develop a grayish haze or opacity in the eyes due to the aging of the lens—an early sign of geriatric cataracts. Even if opaque cataracts occur, surgical removal is possible. However, real treatment for gradual hearing loss does not exist. A preventative is to teach you puppy verbal commands in tandem with hand signals so that he can understand you, even when his hearing goes. Routinely check ear canals to ensure that they are clean and clear.

Incidence of tooth and gum disease increases with age, so good dental care is essential. Hard biscuits and bones can help to remove tartar, but a vet may recommend extracting loose teeth during a dental cleaning.

Due to decreased activity, older dogs require fewer calories. Excess weight gain puts additional strain on aging

CPR

CPR (cardiopulmonary resuscitation) means you are giving your dog artificial respiration and chest compressions simultaneously to get his heart going. It's best to have two people working on your dog—one for the breathing and one for the heart. Check your home veterinary manual or go to www.dogpatch.org/doginfo/cpr.html, one of many good websites for CPR instructions.

Medicating Your Westie

Here's how to give your Westie medications:

Liquids

Get a syringe from your vet. Tuck the syringe neatly down the "cheek pocket" of the dog's mouth, and hold the jaws closed. Squirt the medication into the back of the dog's mouth. Avoid cramming it down his throat; this could force the medication into his lungs by mistake.

Pills

If the medication can be given with food, wrap it in a piece of cheese (I once hid some in a California sushi roll) and he'll probably not notice it. For meds taken on an empty stomach, open the mouth and shove the pill as far down as possible and clamp his muzzle shut briefly. Works like a charm. (A little reassurance and praise for him afterward is a nice gesture.) Also, keep the following in mind with your medications:

- Throw out any old medicine.
- Use all the antibiotics your vet prescribes for your dog, even if you think the dog doesn't need them any more.
- Follow label directions carefully.
- Don't mix medications without first checking with your vet.
- Store medication in its original container.
- Carefully observe your Westie for adverse reactions to any medication.

organs. Too much protein can harm dogs with kidney or liver disease. Discuss special diets for dogs with heart, kidney, or liver disease with you vet. You may need to restrict their salt intake. Any diet change should be gradual. Add small amounts of cooked lean chopped meat or cottage cheese to a senior kibble diet if your dog appears to be losing weight. For an essentially toothless Westie, soak kibble in water or switch to canned or home-cooked food.

Urinary tract difficulties commonly arise in older dogs. Often the kidneys lose the ability to concentrate waste. The dog may drink more water. Bladder-control loss could signal failing kidneys, so take him out more frequently.

Osteoarthritis may occur in the geriatric dog. Indulge your Westie with a soft warm bed away from drafts. Moderate exercise and baby aspirin may help relieve the pain. Consult your vet for additional treatments and dosages. Some vets now prescribe glucosamine, which some commercial dog food companies have added to their senior formulas.

Alternative therapies including acupuncture can relieve arthritic discomfort.

Small fatty tumors or cysts often appear on the skin. These are usually benign, but do keep your vet informed, especially if they increase in size.

Older dogs often adjust poorly to stress. Environment changes can be unsettling. If you travel, choose having someone care for him at home over kenneling. With the proper exercise, diet, and medical care, your geriatric Westie should live comfortably.

SAYING GOOD-BYE

When we first lay eyes on that little bundle of fur and energy, in the back of our minds we are always aware that our time on earth together is finite. However, that knowledge doesn't make it any easier when they leave us. The time arrives too soon. As our dog becomes sicker, even though medication can help ease his pain, the good days dwindle.

Although some dogs will go peacefully and without our help, we have the means to help our well-loved Westie make the transition to death. Even so, there's really no way to prepare us for the emotions ahead. Loving support from friends, family, and other pets can help, but it's never easy to say good-bye.

Whether you remain with your Westie through the procedure, wait until he is asleep to say good-bye, or leave him at the vet is a matter of personal choice. Only you can make the decision that's right for you. Follow your heart and know that you have made the best choice for him. He knows you love him and will understand.

Everyone grieves differently. Some give their pets memorials and bury them in beautiful spots. Others scatter their ashes in meaningful places they shared with them. While some people swear they'll never have another dog, others seek another immediately.

It takes courage to let a new dog into your life. But in time, the sadness will turn to fond memories that envelope your heart and soul, and you just might realize that there is no better memorial to a beloved friend than taking in another of his "family." And you may discover that the endearing, precious qualities that made your beloved Westie who he was on this earth never really die.

APPENDIX
BREED STANDARDS

AKC OFFICIAL BREED STANDARD

General Appearance: The West Highland White Terrier is a small, game, well-balanced hardy looking terrier, exhibiting good showmanship, possessed with no small amount of self-esteem, strongly built, deep in chest and back ribs, with a straight back and powerful hindquarters on muscular legs, and exhibiting in marked degree a great combination of strength and activity. The coat is about two inches long, white in color, hard, with plenty of soft undercoat. The dog should be neatly presented, the longer coat on the back and sides, trimmed to blend into the shorter neck and shoulder coat. Considerable hair is left around the head to act as a frame for the face to yield a typical Westie expression.

Size, Proportion, Substance: The ideal size is eleven inches at the withers for dogs and ten inches for bitches. A slight deviation is acceptable. The Westie is a compact dog, with good balance and substance. The body between the withers and the root of the tail is slightly shorter than the height at the withers. Short-coupled and well boned. *Faults – Over or under height limits. Fine boned.*

Head: Shaped to present a round appearance from the front. Should be in proportion to the body. Expression-Piercing, inquisitive, pert. Eyes-Widely set apart, medium in size, almond shaped, dark brown in color, deep set, sharp and intelligent. Looking from under heavy eyebrows, they give a piercing look. Eye rims are black. Faults- Small, full or light colored eyes. Ears-Small, carried tightly erect, set wide apart, on the top outer edge of the skull. They terminate in a sharp point, and must never be cropped. The hair on the ears is trimmed short and is smooth and velvety, free of fringe at the tips. Black skin pigmentation is preferred. *Faults – Round-pointed, broad, large, ears set closely together, not held tightly erect, or placed too low on the side of the head.*

Skull: Broad, slightly longer than the muzzle. not flat on top but slightly domed between the ears. It gradually tapers to the eyes. There is a defined stop, eyebrows are heavy. *Faults – Long or narrow skull.*

Muzzle: Blunt, slightly shorter than the skull, powerful and gradually tapering to the nose, which is large and black. The jaws are level and powerful. Lip pigment is black. *Faults – Muzzle longer than skull. Nose color other than black.*

Bite: The teeth are large for the size of the dog. There must be six incisor teeth between the canines of both lower and upper jaws. An occasional missing premolar is acceptable. A tight scissors bite with upper incisors slightly overlapping the lower incisors or level mouth is equally acceptable. *Faults – Teeth defective or misaligned. Any incisors missing or several premolars missing. Teeth overshot or undershot.*

Neck, Topline, Body: Neck-Muscular and well set on sloping shoulders. The length of neck should be in proportion to the remainder of the dog. *Fault – Neck too long or too short.*

Topline: Flat and level, both standing and moving. *Fault – High rear, any deviation from above.*

Body: Compact and of good substance. Ribs deep and well arched in the upper half of rib, extending at least to the elbows, and presenting a flattish side appearance. Back ribs of considerable depth, and distance from last rib to upper thigh as short as compatible with free movement of the body. Chest very deep and extending to the elbows, with breadth in proportion to the size of the dog. Loin short, broad and strong. *Faults – Back weak, either too long or too short. Barrel ribs, ribs above elbows.*

Tail: Relatively short, with good substance, and shaped like a carrot. When standing erect it is never extended above the top of the skull. It is covered with hard hair without feather, as straight as possible, carried gaily but not curled over the back. The tail is set on high enough to that the spine does not slope down to it. The tail is never docked. *Faults – Set too low, long, thin, carried at half-mast, or curled over back.*

Forequarter-Angulation, Shoulders: Shoulder blades are well laid back and well knit at the backbone. The shoulder blade should attach to an upper arm of moderate length, and sufficient angle to allow for definite body overhang. *Faults – Steep or loaded shoulders. Upper arm too short or too straight.*

Legs: Forelegs are muscular and well boned. relatively short, but with sufficient length to set the dog up so as not to be too close to the ground. The legs are reasonably straight, and thickly covered with short hard hair. They are set in under the shoulder blades with definite body overhang before them. Height from elbow to withers and elbow to ground should be approximately the same. *Faults – Out at elbows. Iight bone, fiddle-front.*

Feet: Forefeet are larger than the hind ones, are round, proportionate in size, strong, thickly padded; they may properly be turned out slightly. Dewclaws may be removed. Black pigmentation is most desirable on pads of all feet and nails, although nails may lose coloration in older dogs.

Hindquarter-Angulation: Thighs are very muscular, well angulated, not set wide apart, with hock well bent, short, and parallel when viewed from the rear. Legs – Rear legs are muscular and relatively short and sinewy. *Faults – Weak hocks, long hocks, lack of angulation. Cowhocks. Feet-Hind feet are smaller than front feet, and are thickly padded. Dewclaws may be removed.*

Coat: Very important and seldom seen to perfection. Must be double-coated. The head is shaped by plucking the hair, to present the round appearance. The outer coat consists of straight hard white hair, about two inches long, with shorter coat on neck and shoulders, properly blended and trimmed to blend shorter areas into furnishings, which are longer on stomach and legs. The ideal coat is hard, straight and white, but a hard straight coat which may have some wheaten tipping is preferable to a white fluffy or soft coat. Furnishings may be somewhat softer and longer but should never give the appearance of fluff. *Faults – soft coat. Any silkiness or tendency to curl. Any open or single coat, or one which is too short.*

Color: The color is white, as defined by the breed's name. *Faults – Any coat color other than white. Heavy wheaten color.*

Gait: Free, straight and easy all around. It is a distinctive gait, not stilted, but powerful, with reach and drive. In front the leg is freely extended forward by the shoulder. When seen from the front the legs do not move square, but tend to move toward the center of gravity. The hind movement is free, strong and fairly close. The hocks are freely flexed and drawn close under the body, so that when moving off the foot the body is thrown or pushed forward with some force. Overall ability to move is usually best evaluated from the side, and topline remains level. *Faults – Lack of reach in front, and/or drive behind. Stiff, stilted or too wide movement.*

Temperament: Alert, gay, courageous and self-reliant, but friendly. *Faults – Excess timidity or excess pugnacity.*

Approved December 13, 1988
Effective February 1, 1989

OFFICIAL KENNEL CLUB BREED STANDARD

General Appearance and Characteristics: The game, hardy "Westie" presents a compact appearance, with good balance and substance. It is short coupled and well boned. The distance from the withers to the root of the tail is slightly shorter than the distance from the withers to the ground. The West Highland White is alert, gay, courageous and self-reliant while remaining friendly. Its expression is piercing, inquisitive and alert.

Head and Skull: The head is in proportion to the body. The hair on the head may be shaped (plucked) to present a round appearance from the front, but is not necessary.
The skull is broad, in proportion to a powerful jaw, and slightly domed between the ears. It is not too long, gradually tapering to the eyes. There is a defined stop. The blunt, powerful muzzle is slightly shorter than the skull and gradually tapers to the nose.

Teeth: A full complement of large (for the size of the breed), strong, white teeth meet in a scissors bite, with the upper incisors slightly overlapping the lower incisors. Tight scissors or level bites are acceptable. There must be six incisor teeth between the canines of both the lower and upper jaws. An occasional missing premolar is acceptable.
Serious faults: Defective or misaligned teeth. Any missing incisors, or several premolars missing. Overshot or undershot bites.

Eyes: The medium-sized, deep set, almond-shaped eyes are dark brown in color. Looking from under heavy eyebrows, and being widely set apart, they have a piercing look; and are sharp and intelligent. The eye rims are black.
Faults: Eyes too small or too full. Light-colored eyes.

Ears: The small ears terminate in a sharp point, but must never be cropped. They are carried tightly erect and are set wide apart on the top outer edge of the skull. The hair on the ears is short, smooth and velvety, and is free of fringe at the tips. Black skin pigmentation is preferred.
Serious faults: The following ears are very objectionable: round-pointed, drop, broad, very large ears, set too close together, not held erect, placed too low on the side of the head.

Neck: A muscular neck gradually thickens toward its base and is well set on sloping shoulders. The length is in proportion to the whole of the dog.
Faults: Neck too long or too short.

Forequarters: The shoulders are well laid back and well knit at the backbone.
Faults: Steep or loaded shoulders.

Forelegs: The muscular, well-boned forelegs are straight and relatively short, but are of sufficient length so that the dog is not too close to the ground. They are set under the shoulder blades with definite body overhang before them. The distance from the withers to the elbow is approximately the same as the distance from the elbow to the ground. Dewclaws may be removed.
Faults: Too short or too straight upper arm. Out at the elbows. Fiddle front. Light bone.

Body: The body is compact and of good substance. Whether standing or moving, the topline is flat and level. The very deep chest extends to the elbows, with the breadth being in proportion to the size of the dog. The deep ribs are well arched in the upper half, extending at least to the elbows and presenting a flattish side appearance. The back ribs are of considerable depth. The distance from the last rib to the hindquarters is as short as is compatible to allow free movement of the body. The back is straight. The short, broad loins are strong.
Faults: High rear. Weak back. Back too long or too short. Barrel ribs. Ribs too short, above the elbows.

Hindquarters: The hindquarters are powerful and muscular.

Hind Legs: The muscular, sinewy hind legs are relatively short. The muscular, well-angulated thighs are not set wide apart. The hock is well bent. The rear pasterns are short and parallel when viewed from the rear. Dewclaws may be removed.
Faults: Weak hocks. Cow hocks. Long rear pasterns. Lack of angulation.

Feet: The round, strong feet are proportionate in size and thickly padded. The front feet are larger than the hind feet. The front feet may be turned out slightly. Black pigment on the pads and black nails are preferred. Nails may lighten in older dogs.

Tail: The tail is relatively short, but is never docked. When standing erect, the tip is approximately level with the top of the skull, thus maintaining a balanced appearance. It is covered with hard, straight hair, but no feathers. The tail is carried gaily, but not curled over the back. It is set on high enough so that the spine does not slope down to it.
Faults: Tail set too low. Tail too long. Thin. Carried at half-mast or over the back.

Coat: The ideal coat is an integral detail of the breed. A double coat is a necessity. The outer coat consists of straight, hard, white hair about two inches long and free from any curl. The abundant undercoat is short, soft and close, resembling fur in texture. The outer coat is shorter on the neck and shoulders blending into the longer furnishings on the stomach and legs. A hard, straight, white coat with wheaten-colored tips is preferable to a fluffy or soft white coat. The furnishings may be somewhat softer and longer, but must never appear fluffy.
The head may be shaped (by plucking) to present a round appearance and act as a frame for the typical Westie expression, but it is not a necessity. The legs are covered with short, hard hair. The hair on the ears is short, smooth and velvety, and is free of fringe at the tips.
Serious faults: Soft coat. Silkiness or tendency to curl. Coat too short. Single coat.

Color: As defined by the name of the breed, the only acceptable color is white.
Disqualifications: Color other than white. Albinism.

Height: Ideal height, measured at the withers is: 11 inches for dogs; 10 inches for bitches; with a slight deviation being acceptable.
Faults: Over or under height limits.

Gait: The preferred gait is free, straight and easy all around, powerful, with reach and drive. The forelegs are freely extended forward by the shoulder. The hind legs move free, strong and fairly close. The hocks are freely flexed and drawn close under the body so that when moving off the foot, the body is propelled forward with some force. As speed increases, the dog single tracks. While moving, the topline remains level.
Faults: Lack of reach. Lack of drive. Stiff, stifled or too wide movement.

Disqualifications: Unilateral or bilateral cryptorchid. Viciousness or extreme shyness. Color other than white. Albinism.

Revised January 1992

RESOURCES

ASSOCIATIONS AND ORGANIZATIONS

Breed Clubs

American Kennel Club (AKC)
5580 Centerview Drive
Raleigh, NC 27606
Telephone: (919) 233-9767
Fax: (919) 233-3627
E-mail: info@akc.org
www.akc.org

Canadian Kennel Club (CKC)
89 Skyway Avenue, Suite 100
Etobicoke, Ontario M9W 6R4
Telephone: (416) 675-5511
Fax: (416) 675-6506
E-mail: information@ckc.ca

Canadian West Highland White Terrier Club
Secretary: Jim Smith
Email: secretary@canadawestieclub.ca

The Kennel Club
1 Clarges Street
London
W1J 8AB
Telephone: 0870 606 6750
Fax: 0207 518 1058
www.the-kennel-club.org.uk

United Kennel Club (UKC)
100 E. Kilgore Road
Kalamazoo, MI 49002-5584
Telephone: (269) 343-9020
Fax: (269) 343-7037
E-mail: pbickell@ukcdogs.com
www.ukcdogs.com

West Highland White Terrier Club of America (WHWTCA)
Secretary: Nancy Staab
Email:
correspondingsecretary@westieclubamerica.com
www.

The West Highland White Terrier Club (UK)
Secretary: Mrs. B. Wilson
E-mail: thewesthighlandwhiteterrierclub@yahoo.co.uk

Rescue Organizations and Animal Welfare Groups

American Humane Association (AHA)
63 Inverness Drive East
Englewood, CO 80112
Telephone: (303) 792-9900
Fax: 792-5333
www.americanhumane.org

American Society for the Prevention of Cruelty to Animals (ASPCA)
424 E. 92nd Street
New York, NY 10128-6804
Telephone: (212) 876-7700
www.aspca.org

Royal Society for the Prevention of Cruelty to Animals (RSPCA)
Telephone: 0870 3335 999
Fax: 0870 7530 284
www.rspca.org.uk

The Humane Society of the United States (HSUS)
2100 L Street, NW
Washington DC 20037
Telephone: (202) 452-1100
www.hsus.org

Sports

International Agility Link (IAL)
Global Administrator: Steve Drinkwater
E-mail: yunde@powerup.au
www.agilityclick.com/~ial

North American Flyball Association (NAFA)
1400 West Devon Avenue #512
Chicago, IL 60660
Telephone: (800) 318-6312
Fax: (800) 318-6318
www.flyball.org

Veterinary Resources

Academy of Veterinary Homeopathy (AVH)
P.O. Box 9280
Wilmington, DE 19809
Telephone: (866) 652-1590
Fax: (866) 652-1590
E-mail: office@TheAVH.org
www.theavh.org

American Academy of Veterinary Acupuncture (AAVA)
100 Roscommon Drive, Suite 320
Middletown, CT 06457
Telephone: (860) 635-6300
Fax: (860) 635-6400
E-mail: office@aava.org
www.aava.org

American Animal Hospital Association (AAHA)
P.O. Box 150899
Denver, CO 80215-0899
Telephone: (303) 986-2800
Fax: (303) 986-1700
E-mail: info@aahanet.org
www.aahanet.org/index.cfm

American Holistic Veterinary Medical Association (AHVMA)
2218 Old Emmorton Road
Bel Air, MD 21015
Telephone: (410) 569-0795
Fax: (410) 569-2346
E-mail: office@ahvma.org
www.ahvma.org

American Veterinary Medical Association (AVMA)
1931 North Meacham Road – Suite 100
Schaumburg, IL 60173
Telephone: (847) 925-8070
Fax: (847) 925-1329
E-mail: avmainfo@avma.org
www.avma.org

British Veterinary Association (BVA)
7 Mansfield Street
London
W1G 9NQ
Telephone: 020 7636 6541
Fax: 020 7436 2970
E-mail: bvahq@bva.co.uk
www.bva.co.uk

Miscellaneous

Association of Pet Dog Trainers (APDT)
150 Executive Center Drive Box 35
Greenville, SC 29615
Telephone: (800) PET-DOGS
Fax: (864) 331-0767
E-mail: information@apdt.com
www.apdt.com

Delta Society
875 124th Ave NE, Suite 101
Bellevue, WA 98005
Telephone: (425) 226-7357
Fax: (425) 235-1076
E-mail: info@deltasociety.org

Therapy Dogs International (TDI)
88 Bartley Road
Flanders, NJ 07836
Telephone: (973) 252-9800
Fax: (973) 252-7171
E-mail:
www.tdi-dog.org

PUBLICATIONS

Books

Billinghurst, Dr. Ian, *Give Your Dog a Bone,* Self, 1993.
Billinghurst, Dr. Ian, *Grow Your Pups with Bones,* Self, 1998.
Ganz, Sandy, *Tracking from the Ground Up,* Ballwin, MO: Show-me Publications, 1992.
Schultze, Kymythy, *Natural Nutrition for Dogs and Cats: The Ultimate Diet,* Carlsbad, CA: Hay House, 1999.

Magazines

AKC *Family* Dog
American Kennel Club
260 Madison Avenue
New York, NY 10016
Telephone: (800) 490-5675
E-mail: familydog@akc.org
www.akc.org/pubs/familydog

AKC *Gazette*
American Kennel Club
260 Madison Avenue
New York, NY 10016
Telephone: (800) 533-7323
E-mail: gazette@akc.org
www.akc.org/pubs/gazette

Dog & Kennel
Pet Publishing, Inc.
7-L Dundas Circle
Greensboro, NC 27407
Telephone: (336) 292-4272
Fax: (336) 292-4272
E-mail: info@petpublishing.com
www.dogandkennel.com

Dog Fancy
Subscription Department
P.O. Box 53264
Boulder, CO 80322-3264
Telephone: (800) 365-4421
E-mail: barkback@dogfancy.com
www.dogfancy.com

Dogs Monthly
Ascot House
High Street, Ascot,
Berkshire SL5 7JG
United Kingdom
Telephone: 0870 730 8433
Fax: 0870 730 8431
E-mail: admin@rtc-associates.freeserve.co.uk
www.corsini.co.uk/dogsmonthly

WEBSITES

Dog-Play
A cornucopia of information and pertinent links on responsible dog breeding.

The Dog Speaks
Canine Behaviorist Deb Duncan's site, filled with useful advice on canine etiquette, behavior problems, communication, and relevant links.

Petfinder
Search shelters and rescue groups for adoptable pets.

Take Your Dog Tracking
Tracking Judge Allison Platt's page on tracking.

Westie Foundation of America
Covers a wealth of information on health issues that especially concern Westies.

Westie Pedigree Site
A Westie pedigree database.

Westies on the Net
Everything Westie, including active clubs, the WHWTCSEM's great rescue information and tips, a message board, and even a jigsaw puzzle.

BIBLIOGRAPHY

Ackerman, Lowell, DVM, *Dr. Ackerman's Book of West Highland White Terriers*, Neptune City, NJ: TFH Publications, 1997.

Carlson, Delbert G., DVM and James M. Griffin, MD, *Dog Owner's Home Veterinary Handbook*, New York: Howell Book House, 1992.

Cummins, Brian, PhD, *Terriers of Scotland and Ireland: Their History and Development,* Phoenix, AZ: Doral Publishing, 2003.

Faherty, Ruth, *Westies from Head to Tail,* Loveland, CO: Alpine Publications, Inc., 1981

Fogel, Bruce, DVM, *The Encyclopedia of the Dog*, New York: Dorling Kindersly Publishing, Inc., 1995.

Hanks, Lisa, ed., *West Highland White Terrier* (Popular Dog Series, Volume 36), Viejo, CA: Bowtie, Inc., 2004.

Hubbard, Clifford L.B., *The Observer's Book of Dogs,* London: Frederick Warne and Co., Ltd., 1962.

Kern, Kerry, *The New Terrier Handbook,* New York: Barron's Educational Series, Inc., 1988.

Kilcommons, Brian and Sarah Wilson, *Paws to Consider,* New York: Warner Books, 1999.

Martin, Dawn, *A New Owner's Guide to West Highland White Terriers,* Neptune City, NJ: TFH Publications, 2001.

Marvin, John T., *The Book of All Terriers,* New York Howell Book House, Inc., 1976 (revised).

Nicholas, Anna Katherine, *The Book of the West Highland White Terrier,* Neptune City, NJ: TFH Publications, 1993.

Rugaas, Turid, *On Talking Terms With Dogs,* Carlsborg, WA: Legacy By Mail, Inc., 1997.

Ruggles-Smythe, Penelope, *West Highland White Terrier,* Allenhurst, NJ: Kennel Club Books, 2003 (revised American edition).

Sanders, William R. (Sil), *Enthusiastic Tracking: The Step-By-Step Training Manual,* Stanwood, WA, Rime Publications, 1998.

INDEX

seborrhea in, 155
senior dogs and, 175-177
skin allergies in, 156-157
spaying and neutering in, 138-139
special diets in, 71-72
tick control in, 163
vaccinations in, 139-142
veterinarian selection for, 136-138
whipworm in, 165
white shaker dog syndrome (WSS) in, 157
worms and worming in, 163-164
wounds and bleeding control in, 175
Heart disease, 160-161
Heartworms, 164
Heatstroke, 173
Hepatitis, 141
Herbal therapy, 168-170
Hindquarters, 19
History of Westie, 4-13
Holistic medicine, 166
Home-cooked meals, 67
Homeopathy, 170-171
Hookworms, 164-165
Housetraining, 94-97
accidents and, 96
punishment and, 96-97

ID tags and microchipping, 50-51
Immune system function, 148
Indefinite Listing Privilege (ILP) program and, 44
Independent nature of Westie, 24
Inflammatory bowel disease (IBD), 148-149
Insect stings/bites, 174

James I of England, 6
Jogging with your Westie, 131

Keenan, Barbara Worcester, 11
Kennel Club (KC), 11, 16
registering your dog with, 40
Kennel cough, 141
Kibble (dry food), 61-62
Kidney (renal) disease, 149-150
Kindergarten training classes, 97-98
Krabbe's disease, 147-148

Label contents of commercial dog food, 60-61
Lanarkstone Kennels, 20, 25
Leash training, 103-104
Leashes, 48, 103-104
Leave It command, 103
Lee, Rawdon, 15

Legg-Calve-Perthes disease, 150-151
Legs, 15, 19
Leptospirosis, 142
Lifespan of Westie, 27
Liver, portosystemic shunt (PSS) in, 152
Loch Crinan, 7
Lost dogs, 51-52
Ludlow, Mary Lou, 46
Lungs, pulmonary fibrosis in, 152-154
Luxating patella, 151-152
Lyme disease, 142

Maggie Mae, 42, **42**
Malcolm, Edward Donald, 7-8, 15
Male vs. Female, 35
Mange (demodectic and sarcoptic), 163
Martin, Dawn, 12, 131
Marvin, Bea, 11
Marvin, John T., 11, 22
McGuire, Kay, 148
Medication administration tips, 176, **176**
Microchipping, 50-51
Minerals, 71-72
Modern Westie in England, 9
Modern Dog, 15
Molly, 42, **42**
Morvan, 9
Motel/hotel stays with your Westie, 55-56
Mouthing behaviors, 110-111
Moving an injured dog, 174

Nail care, 81-83, **84**
Naming your Westie, 46
National Animal Poison Control Center, 175
National Terrier Show, 11
Neck, 18
Noise phobias, 111-112
North American Flyball Association (NAFA), 121
Nose, 17, 128
Nylabone, 48

Obedience competition, 122
Obesity, 72-73, 160
Orthopedic Foundation for Animals (OFA), 151
Other pets and Westie, 28-29, 47

Pacey, May, 6, 9
Paddy, **10**
Pancreatitis, 161-162

Parasites, 162-164
Parvo, 142
People food for dogs, 68
Pet sitters, 57
Pet stores as source of Westie, 42-44
Pet vs. Show quality dogs, 37
Pheromones, 111
Phobias, 110, 111
Physical therapy, 171-172
Pigmentation of skin, 18, 22
Pittenweem variety, 8
Platt, Allison, 128
Poisoning, 174-175
Poltalloch variety, 7-9
Portosystemic shunt (PSS), 152
Predatory drive, 16
Preparing for your Westie, 33-57
Preservatives and additives in dog food, 61-62, 64
Problem behavior, 105-117
aggression as, 112-113, 114-116, 117
barking as, 105-107
canine behaviorist help with, 116-117
chewing as, 107-108
digging as, 108-109
growling as, 110
mouthing/biting as, 110-111
noise phobias as, 111
pheromones and, 111
phobias and, 110, 111-112
separation anxiety as, 113-114, 116
Professional groomers, 88-89
Propylene glycol, 64
Psychologist, animal, 116-117
Pulmonary fibrosis, 152-154
Punishment and training, 96-97
Puppies, 33-47
adult dog adoption vs., 33-35
AKC registration of, 38, 40
breeders as source of, 35-39
feeding of, 69
fencing for, 45, **45**
first night home for, 46-47
Indefinite Listing Privilege (ILP) program and, 44
introducing of, to other pets, 47
kindergarten training classes for, 97-98
male vs. female, 35
naming, 46
pet stores as source of, 42-44
puppy proofing your home for, 44
rescue organizations as source for, 39-41, **42**
shelters as source of, 42

Note: Boldface numbers indicate illustrations.

Acknowledgements

Sandy Davis, your quick answers to my frequent (and possibly annoying) email requests were more important than you'll ever know. Deb Duncan, you kept me honest in a way that made me grow; you taught me so much—including that there are people *way more opinionated* than I am. Beth Widdows, your tireless work for Westie Rescue is *beyond* inspiring. All purebred rescue groups should clone you. Donna Hegstrom, I would not have known to contact others committed to Westie health concerns—especially Kay McGuire, DVM, who was a tremendous help. What would I have done without Sil Sanders and his great versatility information or without Allison Platt, Tracking Goddess Extraordinaire—and very cool person? Roz Rosenblatt—Rally Ho! Dee Hanna, you always have a smile and kind words for everyone and you made time to talk to me. Mary Lou Ludlow—it's been fun. Thanks to Christine Swingle, Jane Fink, and Wendell Marumoto for your ideas on ARF and natural rearing. Nancy Staab: you made me laugh, you informed me, you've been my "directory assistance," and you've introduced me to Trapper, "the Will Rogers of Westies." Linda Wells and Sally George: your information on handling and conformation was exactly what I needed. David Gignac, *merci* for the benefit of your experience and some Canadian breed history. Thanks, Derek Tattersall for sharing Paddy's and your triumph at Crufts. Lorayne Tennet in New Zealand, you're a networker supreme; you hooked me up with numerous people worldwide including Derek, Marcella Lee, Doreen Lancaster and giving me some good information and for being my friend. Suzanne Renaud, thanks for allowing me to use your beautiful artwork. Also thank you, Lisa Brown (and Suebeth Jordan), Beth Bowling, and Sherron Corner for sharing your stories and pictures. Thank you, Janice Beck, who's ever ready to lend a helping hand when it comes to things terrier. Dawn Martin and Billye and Tom Ward—I'm glad we *finally* connected. Thanks also to Clan Chief Mr. Robin Malcolm (direct descendant of Colonel Malcolm) for answering my letter, and to Westie-l Yahoo! List—and to the many others to whom I am grateful. Oh, and thanks, Diane Morgan, for showing me the ropes. To Maggie and Geordie (my two "Westies of Color" AKA Cairn terriers) and my husband, Larry Holtz: I'm back!

About the Author

Jill Arnel is freelance writer who lives in Oregon. Some of her articles have appeared in *Off-Lead Magazine* and Portland's *Dog Nose News*. She also writes fiction, literary analysis, and essays; designs websites; and does freelance editing and copywriting. A member of The Dog Writers' Association of America and Willamette Writers, she lives with her husband, Larry Holtz and her two terriers, Maggie and Geordie, with whom she has participated (and titled) in Obedience, Earthdog, therapy work, Conformation and more. She has two grown sons.

Photo Credits